CHELTENHAM TO ANDOVER
including the
Tidworth Branch

Vic Mitchell and Keith Smith

MP Middleton Press

Cover picture: Southern Region class N no.31816 runs out of the down platform at Chiseldon with the 2.50pm Andover Junction to Swindon Town on 9th September 1961, the last day of passenger services on the route. (S.C.Nash)

First Published March 2000

ISBN 1 901706 43 5

© Middleton Press, 2000

Design Deborah Esher
Typesetting Jane Detrey

Published by
 Middleton Press
 Easebourne Lane
 Midhurst, West Sussex
 GU29 9AZ
Tel: 01730 813169
Fax: 01730 812601

Printed & bound by Biddles Ltd,
 Guildford and Kings Lynn

CONTENTS

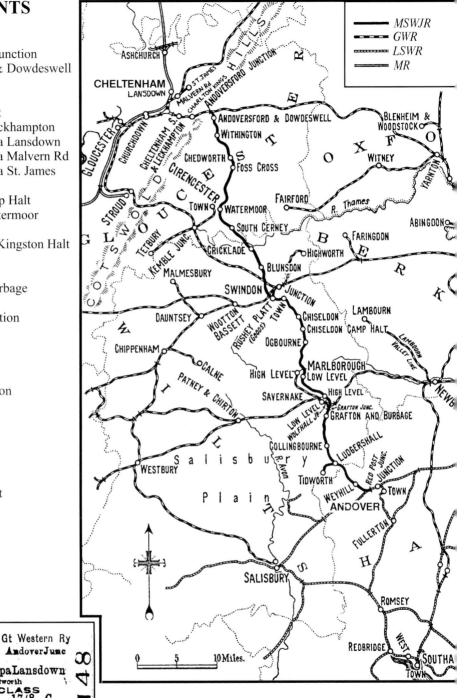

I.   Most of the route was owned by the Midland & South Western Junction Railway until 1923. (Railway Magazine)

ACKNOWLEDGEMENTS

We have received much help and information from many of the photographers mentioned in the captions and also from J.H.Aston, W.R.Burton, G.Croughton, N. Langridge, C.Porter, D.Trevor Rowe, Mr D. & Dr S. Salter, the Signalling Record Society, G.T.V.Stacey, R.E.Toop, R.Wear, Miss M.Wheeller, E.Youldon and our ever supportive wives. To all these we express our sincere gratitude.

GEOGRAPHICAL SETTING

The route runs across a large variety of landforms and geology. Starting at the historic spa town of Cheltenham, the line soon began its climb through the Cotswolds, running close to the west flowing River Chelt east of Charlton Kings. From here to Cirencester the track was mainly on Limestone, which was quarried to benefit the railway's permanent way and also its revenue account.

The summit was near Chedworth and was almost 500ft above sea level. The long descent to South Cerney was partly in the valley of the River Coln. A near level section followed to the outskirts of Swindon. It ran close to the River Churn and other headwaters of the River Thames, in an area composed of clays and gravels, the latter being of some economic importance.

Before entering Swindon Town, the line climbed steeply for a mile. The station was close to the centre of the old town, which was noted for its market. A further climb took the track onto the almost treeless Chalk upland that forms the northern extension of Salisbury Plain, known as the Marlborough Downs.

The route dipped at Marlborough as it crossed the Kennet Valley and before it climbed into the mighty Savernake Forest. A further descent brought it into the Vale of Pewsey, where it passed over the Kennet & Avon Canal.

From Grafton to Andover, the journey was mostly downhill and over Chalk. The Tidworth Branch was also over Chalk, but was steeply graded with a summit near its mid-point.

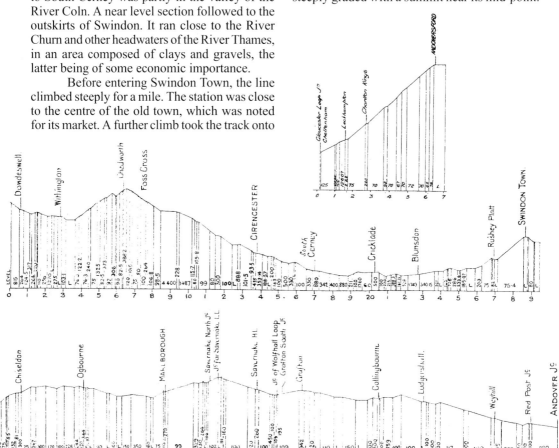

HISTORICAL BACKGROUND

The route appeared late on the railway map and so we look first at the network existing before the line was considered. Cheltenham had a station on the Birmingham & Gloucester Railway from 1840; the station became Lansdown Road and the line part of the Midland Railway. Great Western Railway trains from Gloucester reached Cheltenham in 1844, and began running east from there to Bourton on the Water in 1881.

Further south, Swindon had GWR trains running east, west and north-west from the town from 1840-41, but they ran on broad gauge tracks. GWR services between Newbury and Devizes began operating through Savernake in 1862 and a branch from there to Marlborough was opened in 1864. These lines were broad gauge until 1874.

Andover was served by London & South Western Railway trains from Basingstoke from 1854, these being extended to Salisbury in 1857. The LSWR began running south to Southampton in 1865.

The Swindon, Marlborough & Andover Railway Act was passed on 21st July 1873, but little progress was made with its construction. A fresh start in 1878 resulted in the line between Swindon and Marlborough opening on 27th July 1881. It was built as a single standard gauge line. Trains ran between the SMAR and GWR stations at Swindon between 6th February 1882 and 28th February 1885.

Services between Grafton and Andover began on 1st May 1882, but opening of the Marlborough-Grafton section was delayed until 5th February 1883. The GWR branch from Savernake had to be traversed and this company was particularly intransigent and uncooperative, as the new company was bisecting its territory.

The Swindon & Cheltenham Extension Railway Company's Act received assent on 18th July 1881. This company was amalgamated with the SMAR in 1884 to form the Midland & South Western Junction Railway, the title referring to the two railway giants it was going to link. The line was opened north to Cirencester on 18th December 1883, but Cheltenham trains did not commence until 1st August 1891. Again it was necessary to run over the rails of the distinctly unhelpful GWR; this was for about five miles at the Cheltenham end.

The MSWJR could not survive on the local traffic and the intended business between the Midlands and the South Coast was slow to develop, owing to a combination of long lengths of steeply graded single

track and the antagonism of the GWR causing unpredictable delays. Thus the company was in receivership from 1884 to 1897.

An Act of 7th August 1896 provided for the construction of double track, independent of the GWR, between Marlborough and Grafton, this coming into use on 26th August 1898. The route was doubled between Cheltenham and Cirencester and between Grafton and Weyhill in 1901-02.

For Boer War traffic, the War Department built a line to its Tidworth Camp in 1900. The MSWJR operated it from 1902 (1st July for goods and 1st October for passengers). The branch soon generated more revenue than all the company's other stations combined.

The grouping of the railways in 1923 meant that the MSWJR was swallowed up by its old enemy, the GWR. There were many alterations, including the reintroduction of trains between the two stations in Swindon. Others are described in the captions.

Upon nationalisation in 1948, the route became part of the Western Region of British Railways. However, the Southern Region was responsible for the line from Grafton southwards from April 1950 to February 1958.

Closure to passengers

The Tidworth branch was closed on 17th September 1955 and the 1883 route through Savernake (High Level) was not used after 15th September 1958. Services on the main part of the route, between Andoversford and Andover, ceased on 11th September 1961. The Cheltenham-Andoversford section was in use until 15th October 1962, by trains to Kingham. Freight withdrawals are detailed in the captions. The Andover-Ludgershall section remains in use for military traffic.

Revival

The Swindon & Cricklade Railway was formed in 1978 and a lease was obtained on most of the trackbed between those places. Work started at Blunsdon and a ¾ mile line north to a new station at Hayes Knoll was first used during July 1998; also during weekends the following year. During that time, embankments and bridges were provided on a new alignment south towards Swindon. Local authorities have been supportive of this extension and also of a northward one to Cirencester, although this would involve a new route around Cricklade.

PASSENGER SERVICES

During the first two years, the SMAR operated six weekday and two Sunday trains over its isolated length of line. The figures were five and two after the extension of operation to Andover and to Cirencester. There were some through workings from the LSWR using that company's coaches in 1883-84, but a financial crisis in 1884 brought a drastic cut in services. For two months in 1885, Cirencester saw only one train on weekdays. In 1889, there were two trains north of Swindon and five south thereof on weekdays, with only two southwards on Sundays, plus one to Marlborough.

Completion of the route in 1891, brought four through weekday workings. Only these will be considered in the following notes; examples of the shorter journeys are to be found in the timetable extracts that follow. A train from the MR began to operate over the route to Southampton in 1893 and there were two between 1903 and 1911. The peak year was 1914 when departures from Cheltenham (Queens Road, Lansdown) were at 4.30am "Ocean Boat Express" (Sats. only), 5.15am, 10.37am "South Express", 1.10pm "South Express" (Manchester to Bournemouth), 2.0pm, 5.15pm (to Southampton on Sats.) and 7.20pm. On Sundays there were trains at 5.15am and 3.15pm.

World War I brought a reduction to four through trains, a frequency that still applied in the subsequent conflict. By 1953, this was down to three, with the two Sunday trains just running south of Swindon. There was only one through return journey (worked from Southampton) from 30th June 1958 until cessation of services. Most trains had used Cheltenham Lansdown station, but St.James was the terminus from November 1958.

Tidworth Branch

The down frequency shown below reflects the rapid growth of the camp and the steady usage of the remunerative branch until the impact of improved road transport and reduced military demand.

	Weekdays	Sundays
1902	5	0
1904	9	0
1905	11	6
1914	14	7
1919	7	3
1923	8	1
1939	10	1
1947	8	1
1950	5	0
1951	3	0
1955	3	0

Many trains ran mixed, i.e. goods and passengers, and some worked to and from Andover.

February 1884

SWINDON, MARLBOROUGH & ANDOVER. Timetable extract. Sec., C. L. Brooke. Eng., J. R. Shopland.] [Traff. Man., T. H. Smith.

August 1892

CHELTENHAM, SWINDON, MARLBOROUGH, and ANDOVER.—Midland and South Western Junction. Timetable extract. Gen. Man., Samuel Fay. Sec., A. F. Ranald Daniel. Eng., J. R. Shopland.

SWINDON and MARLBOROUGH.—Swindon, Marlborough, and Andover. [Traffic Man., T. Harrison Smith.

Down.	mrn	mrn	mrn	aft	aft	aft			aft	aft	aft		Up.	mrn	mrn	aft	aft	aft			aft	aft
Swindon Town ....dep	7 20	9 20	1120	1 40	5	07 30			1 30				Marlborough ....dep	8 10	1015	1230	3	8 5	58	3 28		2 50	7 30
Chiseldon	7 30	9 29	1129	1 49	5	9 7 39			2 7	06 40			Ogbourne	8 21	1026	1240	3 19	9 8	39			3 2	7 42
Ogbourne	7 45	9 38	1134	1 5	5	18 7 48			2 20	06 50			Chiseldon	8 29	1035	1249	3 27	9 18	48			3 12	7 51
Marlborough ....arr	8 20	9 48	1149	2	95	29 7 59			2 31	7 2			Swindon Town ....arr	8 38	1044	1257	3 37	9 27	8 57			3 22	8 0

August 1881   June 1920

CHELTENHAM, CIRENCESTER, SWINDON, TIDWORTH, and ANDOVER.—Midland and South Western Junction.

Offices—Swindon.   Sec. and Gen. Man. J. Davies.   Asst. Sec. and Acct., J. S. Liddington.

[Dense timetable — Week Days and Sundays columns]

NOTES.

A Via Romsey and Eastleigh.

b Via Southampton Town.

c Bournemouth West, via Salisbury.

g Except Monday mornings.

v Via Basingstoke.

x Leaves at 12 night on Sundays.

*** Market Street.

† Station for Docks.

‡ New Street.

§ Queen's Road, Lansdown.

‖ Watermoor over ¼ mile to Sheep Street Station (G.W.).

** Cheltenham (South) and Leckhampton.

August 1940. The 1961 timetable is below picture 14.

CHELTENHAM SPA, SWINDON, TIDWORTH, and ANDOVER.

[Dense timetable — Week Days and Sundays columns]

A Lansdown   **Aa** Stops to set down except on Weds. and Sats   **B** Cheltenham (South) and Leckhampton   **b** Sun mrns only   **C** Watermoor   **E** Except Sats.
F About 250 yds to High Level Sta.   **f** Arr 2 54 aft on Sats   **G** Southampton Terminus for Docks   **H** Portsmouth & Southsea   **h** Change at Eastleigh & Fareham. Arr 1 48 aft on Weds. & Sats. changing at Eastleigh   **J** Change at Romsey & Eastleigh   **K** Change at Eastleigh   **k** Arr Savernake 9 17 mrn
L Bournemouth West, via Salisbury, page 167   **p** Stops on Fris. only to take up   **R** Arr. Savernake 7 22 aft   **S** Sats only   **T** High Level Sta   **T&C** Thro Carriage
V Except Weds & Sats   **X** Weds and Sats   **Y** Change at Romsey   **z** Via Leeds (City)

¶ "Halts" at Chiseldon Camp between Chiseldon and Ogbourne; and at Collingbourne Kingston between Grafton & Burbage and Collingbourne

CHELTENHAM SPA ST. JAMES

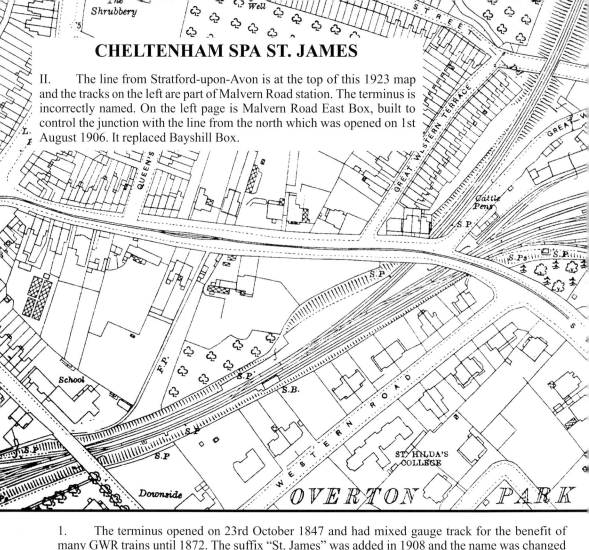

II.   The line from Stratford-upon-Avon is at the top of this 1923 map and the tracks on the left are part of Malvern Road station. The terminus is incorrectly named. On the left page is Malvern Road East Box, built to control the junction with the line from the north which was opened on 1st August 1906. It replaced Bayshill Box.

1.   The terminus opened on 23rd October 1847 and had mixed gauge track for the benefit of many GWR trains until 1872. The suffix "St. James" was added in 1908 and the name was changed to "Cheltenham Spa St. James" in 1925. The exterior was altered little and is seen in 1951. (Lens of Sutton)

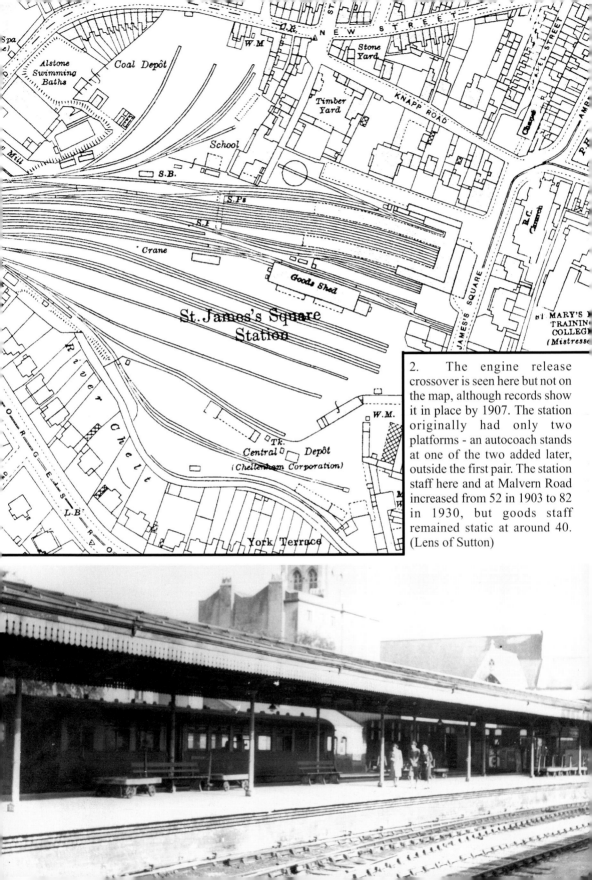

2.   The engine release crossover is seen here but not on the map, although records show it in place by 1907. The station originally had only two platforms - an autocoach stands at one of the two added later, outside the first pair. The station staff here and at Malvern Road increased from 52 in 1903 to 82 in 1930, but goods staff remained static at around 40. (Lens of Sutton)

Map labels:

Alstone Swimming Baths

Coal Depôt

Stone Yard

W.M.

O.R.

NEW STREET

KNAPP ROAD

Timber Yard

School

S.B.

S.Ps

S.I.

Crane

Goods Shed

St. James's Square Station

River Chelt

Tk. Central Depôt (Cheltenham Corporation)

W.M.

L.B.

York Terrace

JAMES'S SQUARE

R.C. Church

St MARY'S TRAINING COLLEGE (Mistresse

3.   Ex-GWR 0-4-2T no. 1413 stands at the platform on 9th October 1954, while ex-SR class U no. 31626 stands close to the turntable. The 53-lever signal box was to the left of it and this was manned until 15th June 1966. Trains on the Andover route used the station only after November 1958. (J.R.W.Kirkby)

4.   Class U 2-6-0 no. 31791 is about to depart at 1.48pm on 9th September 1961 with the last train to Southampton. The station closed to passengers on 3rd January 1966, when the remaining service to Gloucester was withdrawn. Freight continued until that date and coal traffic until 31st October 1966. (S.C.Nash)

Other views can be seen in pictures 104-110 in our *Stratford-upon-Avon to Cheltenham* album.

CHELTENHAM SPA MALVERN ROAD

III.   The tracks on the right overlap those on the left of the previous map and those on the left continue on no. IV. Note that all three show the electric street tramway, which was in use from 1901 until 1930. All trains from Stratford-upon-Avon had to reverse into St. James until this station was opened on 30th March 1908.

5.　　All passengers had to use the footbridge, under which a down train is about to pass. The signal was for trains either reversing to St. James or returning up to the main line. The dock was used for gentlemen's carriages, of the type seen near the entrance. (Lens of Sutton)

6.　　The station was closed as a wartime economy measure from 1st January 1917 to 7th July 1919 and is seen here in June 1951. The Riley will have descended the long inclined drive from Malvern Road. (D.B.Clayton)

7.　　The back of the booking office is on the left and the locomotive coal wagons are level with the lower border of the station signboard. SPA had been added to the name in 1925. (Lens of Sutton)

8.　　On the left is the dock siding, the end of which appears in picture 5. It had been absent for many years, but was relaid in 1942. A southbound train is departing on 1st October 1960 and is passing the 37-lever Malvern Road West Box, which closed on 5th June 1966. However, East Box remained in use until 3rd November 1970. The line was used as an alternative through route to Birmingham from Gloucester until 1976. (H.C.Casserley)

9.   East Box is in the distance as U class no. 31794 runs in with the 1.48pm Cheltenham St.James to Southampton Terminus on 26th August 1961. In the foreground is the short bay platform sometimes used for reversing autotrains running between St. James and stations northwards to Honeybourne. (R.S.Carpenter)

10.   The shed on the right is shown on the map and was erected in 1906 to supersede one that had to be demolished to make way for the junction shown on map II. The shed on the left was erected in 1943. Standing near it on 1st September 1961 is no. 5910 *Park Hall* and on the right is U class no. 31618. The depot closed on 2nd March 1964. (J.J.Smith)

More pictures of this station and its shed can be found in *Stratford-upon-Avon to Cheltenham*.

11.   A westward view from the bridge seen in picture 9 includes the bay platform from which the track was removed in 1965. The station closed to passengers and goods on 3rd January 1966, but the yard continued to be used for wagon storage, as seen. The main water tank is above the coal stage, in the background. (R.A.S.Marketing)

CHELTENHAM SPA
LANSDOWN

Sunningend
(Engineering & Ship Dec...

Tk
Tramway Depot

W.M

S.P.

S.P.

Wes.Meth.
Chapel

B.M.180.1

302ª
·542

S.B.

S.P.

S.P.

Hall

Inst.

School

R O M A N   R O A D

A L B E R T U S   R O A D

S.P.

T R A M W A Y

G — L — O — U — C

S.P.

P.H.

P.O.

B.M.180·4

S.B.

Lansdown
Station

S.P.

S.P.

S.P.

S.P.

S.P.

ELDORADO RO

S.P.

KENSINGTON AVENUE

S.P.

ERN PARK ROAD

IV. The 1923 edition has the former Midland Railway main line from top to bottom and part of the Malvern Road trackwork on the right. Work started in 1890 to enlarge the facilities to accommodate MSWJR trains. The new carriage sidings and turntable are top right; goods sidings and an engine shed were built further north, near the old High Street station.

12. A southbound train, headed by MR 4-2-2 no. 133, has a horsebox behind the engine. In the bay platform is a MSWJR train, destined for Swindon Town, or beyond. (R.M.Casserley coll.)

13. Unless proceeding promptly after leaving the carriage sidings, MSWJR trains started from the bay platform, as seen. No. 23 was built by Beyer Peacock in 1899, as part of a batch of ten, and ran until 1937, but it lost its fine scroll lettering in 1923. (R.C.Riley coll.)

14. The grand, albeit neglected, south-east elevation was photographed in the 1930s. Note the small porte-cochere on the right. This decade saw ticket sales for the route plummet from 6000 to almost 3000. (Mowat coll.)

CHELTENHAM SPA, SWINDON and ANDOVER JUNCTION

Miles		Week Days															Suns	
		am Mondays to Fridays	am	am	am	am	am	pm Saturdays only	pm Saturdays only Through Train Cheltenham to Southampton Terminus	pm Mondays to Fridays Through Train Cheltenham to Southampton Terminus	pm	pm	pm Mondays to Fridays	pm	pm Mondays to Fridays	pm	am	pm
—	**Cheltenham Spa** (St James') dep		6 30	..	..	9 50	1050	..	1 48	1 52	2 25	..	..	5 50	..	6 28	..	..
½	**Cheltenham Spa** (Malvern Rd.) „		..	..	..	9 52	1052	..	1 50	1 55	2 27	..	..	5 52	..	6 30	..	..
3	Cheltenham Leckhampton		6 37	..	..	9 59	1058	..	1 57	2 1	2 33	..	..	5 58	..	6 36	..	..
4¼	Charlton Kings		6 42	..	..	10 4	11 3	..	..	..	2 38	..	..	6 3	..	6 41	..	..
8	Andoversford		6 52	..	..	1012	1112	..	2 10	2 14	2 47	..	..	6 12	..	6 50	..	..
11	Withington Halt		..	..	..	..	..	..	2 17	2 20	..	..		..	..	..	..	..
14½	Chedworth Halt		..	..	..	..	..	..	2 27	2 30	..	..		..	..	..	..	..
15¾	Foss Cross		..	..	..	..	..	..	2 31	2 33	..	..		..	..	..	..	..
22	**Cirencester** (Watermoor)	6 34	..	..	..	..	..	..	2 45	2 45	..	..		..	7 10	..	..	..
25	South Cerney	6 40	..	..	..	..	..	..	2 52	2 52	..	..		..	7 17	..	..	..
28½	Cricklade	6 49	..	..	..	..	..	..	3 0	3 0	..	..		..	7 24	..	..	..
36¾	**Swindon Town** arr	7 3	..	..	..	..	..	..	3 15	3 15	..	..		..	7 38	..	..	..
39¾	**Swindon** arr	7 15	..	..	..	..	..	..	..	..	..	..		..		..	..	..
—	Mls **Swindon** dep	..	..	7 4	..	..	..	1 5	..	..	..	..	5 55	..		..	9 35	5 45
—	3 **Swindon Town** arr	..	..	7 18	..	..	..	1 14	..	..	..	..	6 3	..		..	9 43	5 53
—	**Swindon Town** dep	..	..	7 22	8 9	..	..	1 15	3 19	3 19	..	4 52	6 7	..		..	9 50	5 55
40	Chiseldon	..	..	7 32	8 17	..	..	1 24	3 27	3 27	..	5 0	6 15	..		..	9 58	6 3
41¼	Chiseldon Camp Halt	..	..	7 36	..	..	..	1 28	3 30	3 30	..	5 3	..	..		..	..	..
43½	Ogbourne	..	..	7 42	..	..	..	1 35	3 36	3 36	..	5 9	..	..		..	10 7	..
48	**Marlborough** arr	..	..	7 52	..	..	..	1 49	3 46	3 46	..	5 19	..	..		..	10 16	6 22
	Marlborough dep	..	..	7 55	..	..	..		3 51	3 48	..	5 20	..	..	..	..	10 18	6 23
53	Savernake (Low Level) arr	..	..	8 7	..	..	..		4 2	3 59	..	5 31	..	..	..	..	10 29	6 34
	Savernake (Low Level) dep	..	..	8 28	..	..	..		4 4	4 1	..	5 32	..	..	..	..	10 31	6 35
55	Grafton and Burbage	..	..	8 35	..	..	..		4 10	4 7	..	5 38	..	..	..	..	10 37	6 41
58	Collingbourne Kingston Halt	..	..	8 41	..	..	..		4 15	4 12	..	5 43	..	..	..	..	10 41	6 45
59¼	Collingbourne	..	..	8 45	..	..	..		4 18	4 15	..	5 47	..	..	..	..	10 45	6 49
61¾	Ludgershall	..	..	8 53	..	..	..		4 25	4 22	..	5 53	..	..	..	..	10 52	6 55
65¾	Weyhill	..	..	9 1	..	..	..	..	4 33	4 30	..	6 1	..	..	..	..	11 0	7 3
69¼	**Andover Junction** arr	..	..	9 8	..	..	..	..	4 41	4 38	..	6 9	..	..	..	..	11 8	7 12
95½	**32, 54** Southampton Central arr	..	..	10E49	..	..	..	..	5 28	5 27	..	7 32	..	..	..	..	12 19	8 19
97¼	**32, 54** Southampton Terminus „	..	..	10SX47	..	..	..	..	5 36	5 37	..	7SO47	..	..	..	..	..	..
122	**54** Portsmouth and Southsea „	..	..	11 16	..	..	..	..	6 16	6 14	..	8C12	..	..	..	..	12 47	8 53
119	**32** Bournemouth Central „	..	..	12 9	..	..	..	..	6 40	6 26	..	8K37	..	..	..	..	1 42	9 24
86¾	**35** Salisbury „	..	..	10B 3	..	..	..	..	5 57	5 57	..	7 0	..	..	..	..	11 51	7 42
136	**35** **London** (Waterloo) „	..	..	11 8	..	..	..	..	6 13	6 33	..	8A 6	..	..	..	..	3 49	9 8

A On Saturdays arr 8 10 pm
B On Saturdays arr 9 42 am

C On Saturdays arr 8 16 pm
E On Saturdays arr 11 3 am
K On Fridays arr 8 29 pm

SO Saturdays only
SX Mondays to Fridays

September 1961

15.   The former MSWJR High Street shed is seen in 1931; the company had ten sidings to the left of it, plus two short ones. The first single-road wooden shed was completed in 1893, and was replaced by this structure in 1911, which remained in use until December 1935. The allocation in 1923 comprised six 4-4-0s, five 0-6-0s, two 2-4-0s and one 4-4-4T.   (R.C.Riley coll.)

16.   A 1947 view across the former MSWJR bay includes the two through platforms, a horse box and an ex-US Army lorry. The dual profile loading gauge was unknown further south.   (R.M.Casserley coll.)

17.   A southward panorama from 1960 includes the footbridge and its novel short length roof. MSWJR trains used to arrive on the right and then proceed to the carriage sidings. The locomotive would be turned, reversed to the shed for servicing and then run forward, past the train and then back onto it. (H.C.Casserley)

18.   The station is in the distance as "Patriot" class no. 45504 *Royal Signals* runs towards Gloucester on 9th September 1961. It is approaching Lansdown Junction. The station and two carriage sidings were still in use nearly 40 years later. (S.C.Nash)

LANSDOWN JUNCTION

V.   The top of this map continues from the bottom of the previous one and includes the tramway terminus. This simple junction arrangement lasted until August 1942, when the route shown diagonally was quadrupled for wartime traffic. Andover trains used the Banbury line, and connections were provided between it and all four tracks. The junction was triangular between 1906 and 1956, the southern part carrying a Swindon Town-Gloucester freight service for many years. It was known as Hatherley Curve.

19.   A photograph from 9th September 1961 shows U class no. 31791 having just passed under the original arch of the road bridge with the 7.50am from Andover Junction to Cheltenham Spa St. James. The lines to Lansdown are on the right and the junction is beyond the bridge. This was altered in November 1958 and prevented Andover trains reaching Lansdown. Former SR locomotives were introduced to the route in 1953. (S.C.Nash)

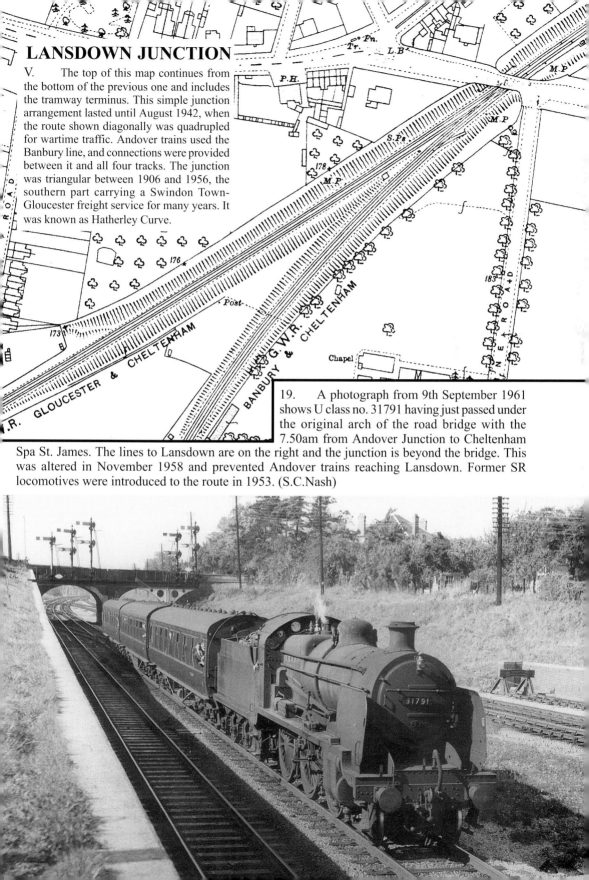

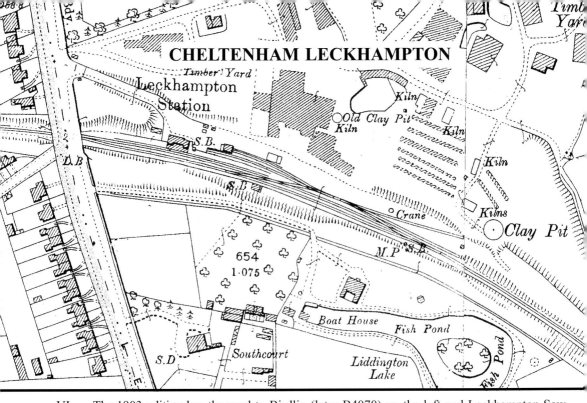

CHELTENHAM LECKHAMPTON

Timber Yard

Leckhampton Station

Timber Yard

S.B.

L.B.

S.B.

Old Clay Pit
Kiln
Kiln

Kiln

Kiln

Crane

Kilns

654
1·075

M.P S.B.

Clay Pit

Boat House   Fish Pond

S.D

Southcourt

Liddington Lake

Fish Pond

VI.   The 1903 edition has the road to Birdlip (later B4070) on the left and Leckhampton Saw Mills & Brick Works on the right. The survey must have been undertaken shortly before the doubling of the Lansdown Junction to Andoversford section, which was opened to traffic on 28th September 1902.

20.   Opened as "Leckhampton" on 1st June 1881, the name was changed to "Cheltenham (South) & Leckhampton" in May 1906. The final change to "Cheltenham Leckhampton" took place in April 1952. The train is on a 1 in 77 down gradient. There were three or four men employed here between the wars. (Lens of Sutton)

21. The main building was on the north side of the line and remained little changed before its closure on 15th October 1962 (to both passengers and goods). In that year, there were six trains calling in each direction, weekdays only. (Lens of Sutton)

22. The lengthy platforms were necessary for the long distance trains that did not call at any other Cheltenham station. There was a weekday Newcastle-upon-Tyne to Swansea train stopping here for many years. It carried through coaches from Hull and ran via Sheffield, Rugby and Banbury, the former Great Central route. It also called at Chepstow, Newport, Cardiff and Barry Docks; thus it was of value to mariners changing ships. This eastward view is from 1960 and includes the signal box, which had 23 levers and remained in use until line closure. (E.Wilmshurst)

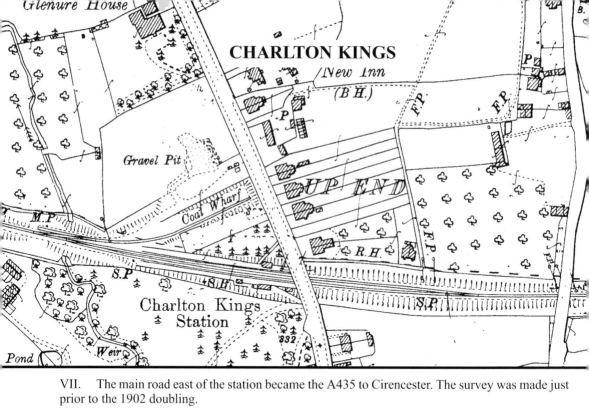

VII.   The main road east of the station became the A435 to Cirencester. The survey was made just prior to the 1902 doubling.

23.   Looking east in September 1923, with the station in the distance, we have the new 1¼ mile long line to Leckhampton Quarry on the right. It climbed 450ft. but closed in November 1926, following bankruptcy of the operators. (H.G.W.Household)

24.	This westward view includes the 1902 signal box, which was close to a crossover and the points to the goods yard, which closed on 1st December 1954. The box was closed on 30th January 1955. There was a staff of four in the early 1930s. (Lens of Sutton)

25.	The station ceased to be staffed after 9th April 1956 and was photographed from an eastbound train in the following month. It closed completely on 15th October 1962. Three miles east of the station was the 384yds long Andoversford Tunnel, which passed under Sandywell Park. (H.C.Casserley)

ANDOVERSFORD JUNCTION

VIII.   The line from Charlton Kings (left) was doubled on 9th February 1902 and a goods loop was provided on the approach to the station, near Station Box. This box was built in 1881 and replaced in 1935. Junction Box was added in 1891. Both were closed on 15th October 1962. The main road became the A40 in 1919. The embankment linking the lower part of both pages was intended to carry the line on an easier curve, avoiding the station. Note the proximity of the cattle market. The number of wagons of livestock dropped from 596 in 1930 to 292 in 1938. Over the same period, tickets issued fell from 6138 to 2172 and freight tonnage from 10,593 to 5964.

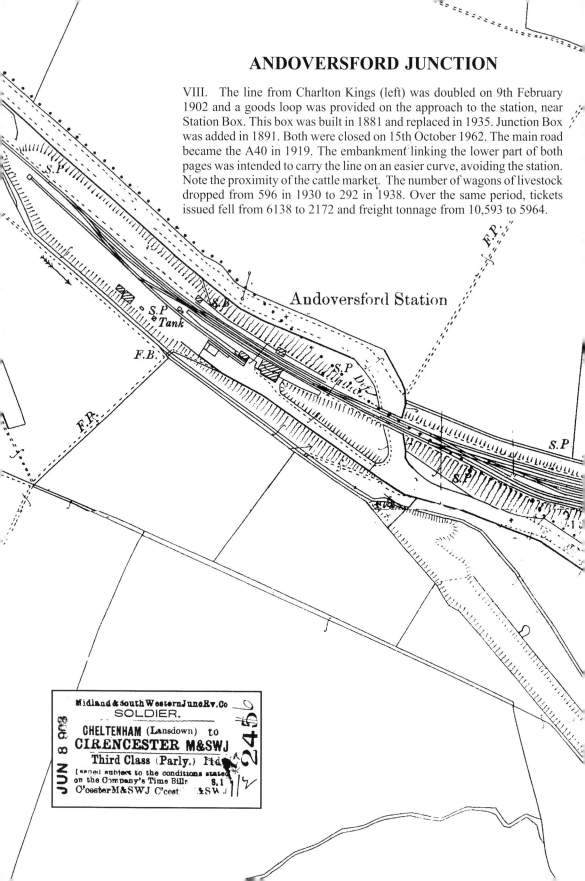

Andoversford Station

Midland & South Western Junc Ry. Co
SOLDIER.
CHELTENHAM (Lansdown) to
CIRENCESTER M&SWJ
Third Class (Parly.) ﬅd
[ssued subject to the conditions stated
on the Company's Time Bill: 8,1
C'cester M&SWJ C'cest   &S W J

JUN 8 90?
245

26.   The junction signals and the Cotswolds are in the distance in this eastward view. The ground signal allowed reversal into the goods yard, which closed on 15th October 1962. The manning level was 7 to 9 between the wars. (R.M.Casserley coll.)

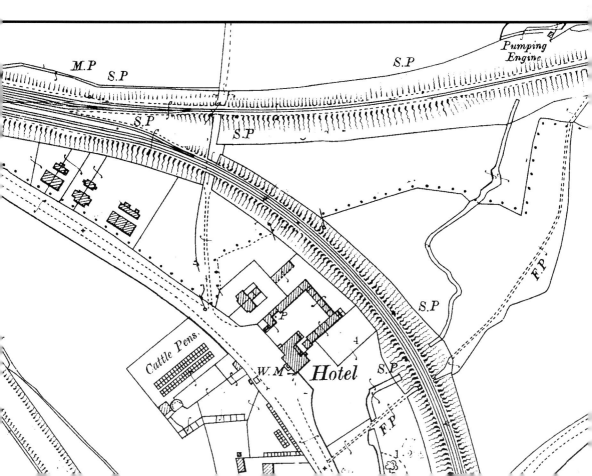

27.　　No. 31618 is about to pass over the junction points on 1st September 1961 and to turn south, leaving former GWR metals and reaching the commencement of the ex-MSWJR route. The vindictive GWR did not allow MSWJR trains to stop at their station until 1904, much to the inconvenience of east-south passengers. (J.J.Smith)

28.　　Junction Box is just visible beyond the A40 bridge. The Andover route curves right, the tracks being linked by a crossover since 9th July 1928, when single line working was introduced. The former southbound track was used for passenger services, the other one functioning as a siding to the next station until 5th October 1962. (D.B.Clayton)

29.　　In the foreground are the two exchange sidings, once used by the two uncooperative companies. The many point rods run to Junction Box, which is beyond the right border of the picture. (A.E.Bennett)

ANDOVERSFORD AND DOWDESWELL

IX.   The 1903 map reveals that while the gate to the goods yard was close to the Police Station and the village centre, the passenger station was much further south. Goods traffic commenced on 16th March 1891, but passenger services did not begin until 1st August of that year, as the junction was not complete. An engine shed was in use here until 1893, when the one at Cheltenham High Street was ready. In 1923, there was a staff of three that issued 1590 tickets (plus 7 seasons) and handled 2467 tons of goods.

F.B.

Ford

S.P.

G.P. Smithy

Police Station

F.W.

Royal Oak Inn

Goods Shed

M.P. { Cheltenham ___ 6
        { Oxford ___ 33

S.P.

S.P.

61
1·78

F.

Old Sa

Andoversford & Dowde
Station

River Coln

C.R.

F.P.

S.B.

S.P.

S.P.

F.

30.   The station was simply "Dowdeswell" until 1st October 1892. A southward panorama includes double track; this was single until 2nd September 1900 and from 9th July 1928. The route northwards was double from the opening. The signal box closed on 8th July 1928. (R.M.Casserley coll.)

31.   Passenger trains ceased to call after 1st April 1927, but the goods yard remained open until 15th October 1962. It had been accessed by a half mile long siding from Andoversford Junction since 9th July 1928, this having been previously the northbound running line. The yard points are seen in 1935, by which time the building was serving travellers on the A40. (NRM)

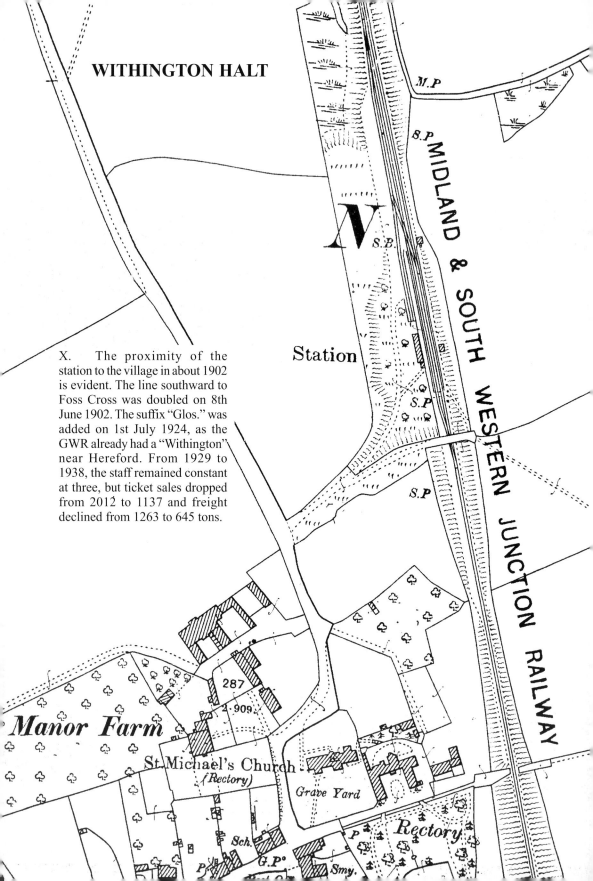

WITHINGTON HALT

X. The proximity of the station to the village in about 1902 is evident. The line southward to Foss Cross was doubled on 8th June 1902. The suffix "Glos." was added on 1st July 1924, as the GWR already had a "Withington" near Hereford. From 1929 to 1938, the staff remained constant at three, but ticket sales dropped from 2012 to 1137 and freight declined from 1263 to 645 tons.

Station

MIDLAND & SOUTH WESTERN JUNCTION RAILWAY

M.P

S.P

S.P

S.P

S.P

287

.909

Manor Farm

St. Michael's Church

(Rectory)

Grave Yard

Rectory

Sch.

G.P°

Smy.

32.   A look northwards from the occupation bridge reveals a layout typical of so many minor rural stations, the goods yard being linked to both running lines with trailing points. The route was singled in 1928, but a loop was retained until 1957. It had to be extended northwards in 1942 for wartime traffic. (Lens of Sutton)

33.   The 14-lever signal box was in use until 1956, but remained as a ground frame until 24th November 1957. Staffing ceased and goods traffic was withdrawn on 28th May 1956, when it became a halt. Only the sign and some posters indicate that it was still open. It remained so until the route closed, by which time the population was 458. (Lens of Sutton)

NORTH OF CHEDWORTH

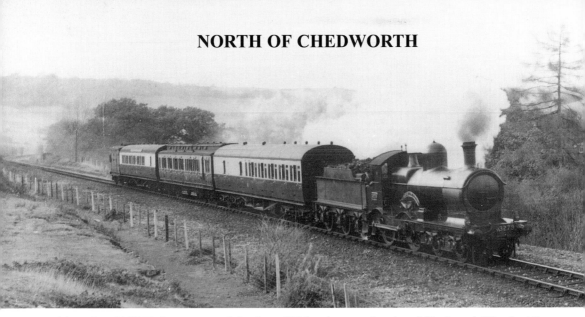

34.   No. 3279 *Torbay* runs south in about 1935 and passes the site of Chedworth Woods sidings. There were two in use in the foreground between 1919 and 1923, the points being secured electrically from Withington Box. They were planned in 1918 to meet wartime needs and could accommodate 40 wagons. (R.S.Carpenter coll.)

CHEDWORTH HALT

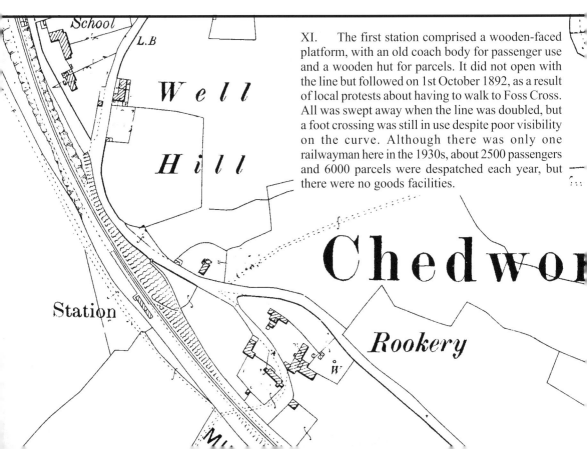

XI.   The first station comprised a wooden-faced platform, with an old coach body for passenger use and a wooden hut for parcels. It did not open with the line but followed on 1st October 1892, as a result of local protests about having to walk to Foss Cross. All was swept away when the line was doubled, but a foot crossing was still in use despite poor visibility on the curve. Although there was only one railwayman here in the 1930s, about 2500 passengers and 6000 parcels were despatched each year, but there were no goods facilities.

35. The shelter on the left appears to be the former parcels shed, repositioned and with doors removed. The new platforms were further north than the original one, the entrance being from the lane to the school. (Lens of Sutton)

36. The signal box had 14 levers, but only 10 in use, and controlled two crossovers and access to a short temporary siding to the south of it. The box was in use between 1902 and 1928, the double track period. The need to widen the cutting made this an expensive station. (Lens of Sutton)

37. Now we look south in 1950. The station served a community of about 720 at that time and became an unstaffed halt on 1st February 1954. North of the station was the 494yd-long Chedworth Tunnel; south of the platforms was the summit of the route - 637ft above sea level. There was only one passenger train each way for the final three years, from this and the neighbouring stations. (LGRP/NRM)

FOSS CROSS

XII. This windswept upland location was a good place for a passing loop on the original single line, being halfway between Withington and Cirencester, but a bad place for passenger revenue. There were very few dwellings within a mile, but income from agricultural traffic compensated. A cattle pen was erected in 1911. The name originated from crossroads on the Roman Foss Way, half a mile distant. The upper line on the right ran to a limestone quarry and the two on the left at the bottom did likewise. From 1930 to 1938, minerals despatched fell from 12,400 to 2400 tons, passengers from 1442 to 440 and wagons of livestock from 64 to 10.

S.P.

S.P.

S.B.

Foss Cross Station

S.P.

W.M.

S.P.

JUNCTION RAILWAY

Engine Shed

297

Gt. Western Ry.	Gt. Western Ry
Withington(Glos	Withington(Glos
TO	
FOSS CROSS	
THIRD CLASS	
9d C Fare 9d C	
Foss Cross	FossCross
FOR CONDITIONS SEE BACK J.D.	

297

38.   A northward view features the signal box, which had 18 working levers and 4 spare in 1923. The points for the goods loop can be discerned. On Market Mondays only, for much of the 1928-31 period, a train from Gloucester terminated here at 8.40am and returned there 30 minutes later. It was a rare example of a train not running into Cheltenham from this route. (Lens of Suttton)

39.   The south end of the goods loop is seen in 1960. The sidings had been extended in 1920, owing to the increased amounts of stone for railway ballast and building purposes being loaded here. (H.C.Casserley)

CIRENCESTER WATERMOOR

School

CHURCH

Roman
Sculptured
Stone. Coins
ery found

QUEEN STREET

W

Abl

P

F.P.

Ps.

P

P

SCHOOL LANE

Watermoor
Villa

PARADE

P

P

ROAD

P

P

W

W

n Coins &
ery found

P

P

Roman
Coins found

P

P

ROMAN GATE
(Site of)

P

Roman Sep
Monuments

CITY

WALL (Site of)

S.P

P.H.

Allotment
Gardens

S.P

Mission Room

shd

Cattle
Pens

Goods
Shed

S.P

P

Allotment
Gardens

Horse & Dril
(P.H.)

M.P

Station

Engine House

S.B.

P

S.P

P

GAS LANE

P

P

Gas Works

S.P

P

Infectious
Diseases
Hospital

Allotm

XIII This survey was made just before the new double track from the north was connected on 12th July 1901. The large buildings on the left provided all the works facilities for the MSWJR, the stores being adjacent to Gas Lane. Above "Engine House" is the wagon repair shop. One locomotive was normally allocated here and used for freight traffic. The shed and adjacent turntable ceased to be used regularly after March 1924. In 1929, 12,431 tickets were issued (in addition to 103 seasons) and over 22,000 tons of goods were handled.

40.   The tallest building in this northward panorama is the former locomotive repair shop. The goods shed is in the centre and a grey coal wagon stands in the dock siding, in which there was a weighbridge. This picture is from 1956. The average tonnage of coal arriving in the 1930s was 7428 per annum. (R.M.Casserley)

41.   The name "Watermoor" was added on 1st July 1924, the GWR already having another station here, which became "Town". This southward view from about 1935 includes the gasworks, which had a private siding from 28th September 1892. Established in 1833, the works had previously received coal via the adjacent canal. Around 5000 tons was used each year until closure in 1939. The station has vanished and has been replaced by a roundabout and new roads.
(Brunel University Transport coll.)

42.   The works were established here in 1895, extended westwards in 1915 and closed on 26th October 1925. The main building had an overhead travelling crane. The 1915 machine shop is on the left and the carriage and paint shop was behind it. There was a staff of 85 in 1923, many of whom travelled to Swindon Works after the closure. An extra train was run; the fare was ½d . This was the sad scene in 1960. Freight continued until 1st April 1964. (I.D.Beale)

43.   The signal box had 19 levers and was closed on 21st August 1960. The house beyond the water tank was clad entirely with corrugated iron and was used successively by the stationmaster, the locomotive superintendent and the civil engineer. U class no. 31620 is about to depart south, in about 1959. The up platform was not used after about March 1960, owing to the bridge at its far end having been damaged by a tall vehicle trying to pass under it. (C.L.Caddy coll.)

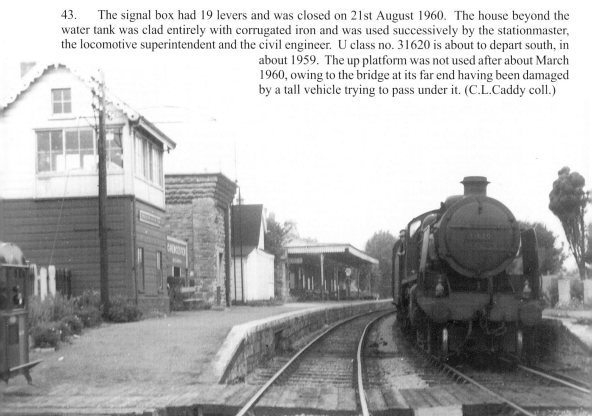

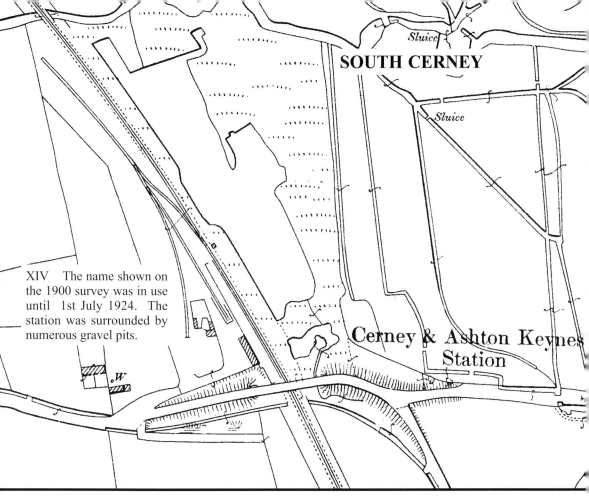

SOUTH CERNEY

Sluice

Sluice

XIV   The name shown on the 1900 survey was in use until 1st July 1924. The station was surrounded by numerous gravel pits.

Cerney & Ashton Keynes Station

.*W*

44.   The route between Cirencester and Marlborough was never doubled, but a passing loop was added here in September 1900. The original platform was narrowed and an extra one constructed. Around 3000 tickets were issued each year in the 1930s, but minerals despatched fluctuated greatly - 845 tons in 1929, 418 in 1936 but under 70 in the other years. (Lens of Sutton)

45.   Seen from the same viewpoint on the bridge is the passing loop and typical access to the goods yard. The signal box gradually became obscured by creepers; it contained 14 levers, all of which were in use. (Lens of Sutton)

46.   The GWR built a new signal box in 1942, as the loop had to be lengthened southwards to accommodate the longer wartime trains. It had a 28-lever frame, but there were six spaces. Its status was as a ground frame from September 1961 to March 1964. (H.C.Casserley)

2nd · SINGLE   SINGLE · 2nd
Cirencester Watermoor to
CIRENCESTER W   CIRENCESTER W
S'th Cerney   S'th Cerney
SOUTH CERNEY
(W)   3d.   FARE   3d.   (W)
For conditions see over For conditions see over

47.   No. 3203 approaches the new rodding tunnel under the platform, with freight from Cheltenham.   Goods traffic at the station continued until 1st July 1963, gravel being a significant part of it for many years.
(E.Wilmshurst)

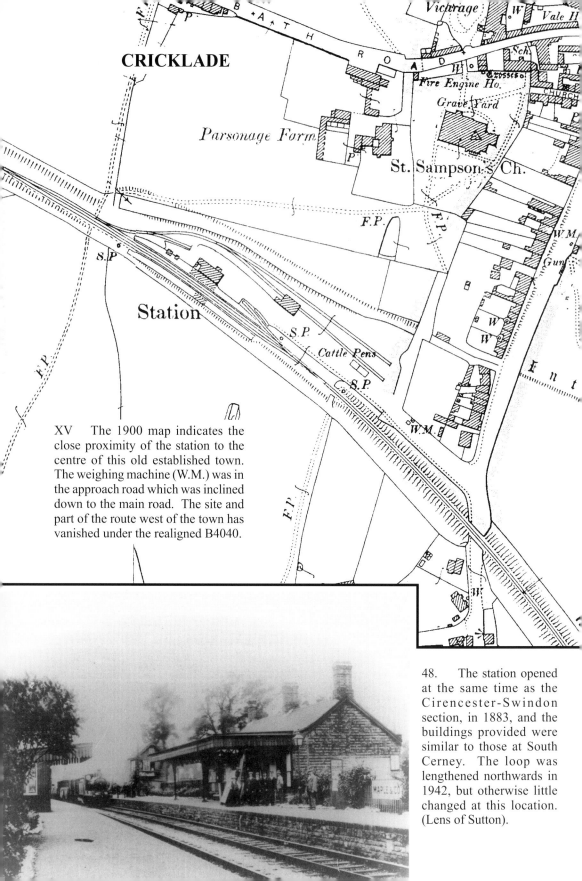

CRICKLADE

Parsonage Farm

St. Sampson's Ch.

Vicarage

Fire Engine Ho.

Grave Yard

Station

Cattle Pens

XV   The 1900 map indicates the close proximity of the station to the centre of this old established town. The weighing machine (W.M.) was in the approach road which was inclined down to the main road. The site and part of the route west of the town has vanished under the realigned B4040.

48.   The station opened at the same time as the Cirencester-Swindon section, in 1883, and the buildings provided were similar to those at South Cerney. The loop was lengthened northwards in 1942, but otherwise little changed at this location. (Lens of Sutton).

49.   Docks were provided for traffic in both directions and a new weighbridge for carts was installed near the cattle dock. Goods inward was notably coal for the local population, which had reached almost 2000 by the time the line closed. A camping coach arrived in 1941 for use by land reclamation labourers. (Stations UK)

50.   The signal box, which had 14 levers, remained little changed, but was reduced to a ground frame from the end of passenger services until 1st July 1963, when goods traffic ceased. There was always a substantial milk transhipment here. For 1931 the figures for parcels and churns totalled 7717, tickets issued were 5208 and total goods 7106 tons. (R.M.Casserley coll.)

HAYES KNOLL

51.   A new station with engine shed attached, has been created by the SCR, more than a mile south of Cricklade. Vast volunteer effort has been forth-coming and this was the southward view in January 1996 as work progressed. The first locomotive entered the shed on 1st August 1999. (M.J.Stretton)

52.   The signal box was built by the GWR for Rowley Regis in Staffordshire in 1887. However, the 30-lever frame came from Totnes in Devon. (P.G.Barnes)

→

53.   The passenger platform was officially opened on 5th December 1999 and was photographed in March of that year. There is no public access to the site, other than by train. (P.G.Barnes)

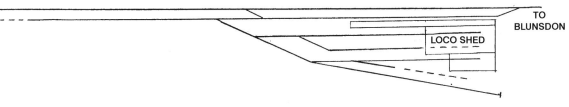

TO
BLUNSDON

LOCO SHED

XVI. The track diagram shows the layout in 1999, with projected lines indicated with dashes.

BLUNSDON

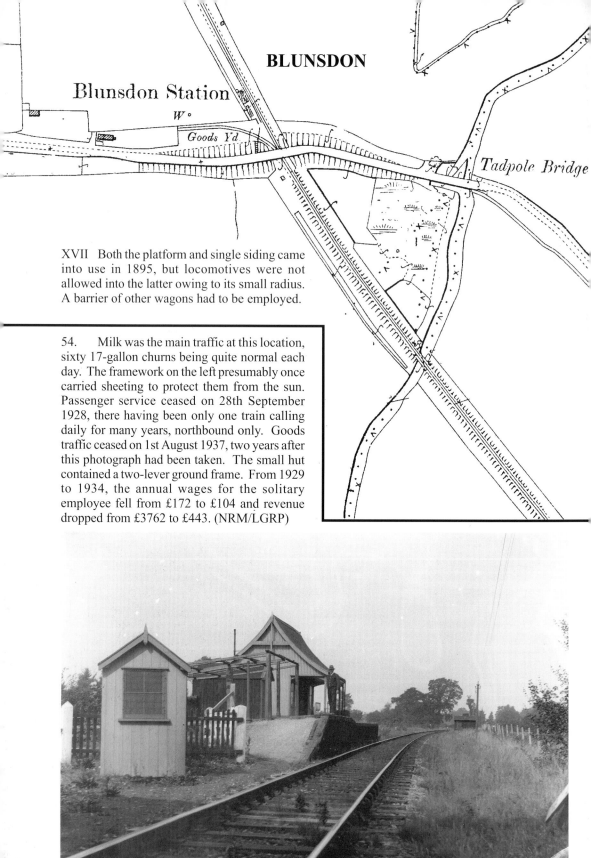

Blunsdon Station

W °

Goods Yd.

Tadpole Bridge

XVII Both the platform and single siding came into use in 1895, but locomotives were not allowed into the latter owing to its small radius. A barrier of other wagons had to be employed.

54.   Milk was the main traffic at this location, sixty 17-gallon churns being quite normal each day. The framework on the left presumably once carried sheeting to protect them from the sun. Passenger service ceased on 28th September 1928, there having been only one train calling daily for many years, northbound only. Goods traffic ceased on 1st August 1937, two years after this photograph had been taken. The small hut contained a two-lever ground frame. From 1929 to 1934, the annual wages for the solitary employee fell from £172 to £104 and revenue dropped from £3762 to £443. (NRM/LGRP)

55.   We now have two views from the road bridge in May 1999. The hut seen in the previous picture would have been in the centre foreground of this photograph. The locomotive had previously been BR no. D2022, a class 03 diesel of 1958. (V.Mitchell)

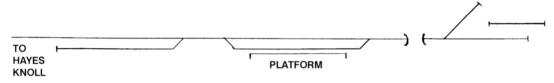

TO
HAYES
KNOLL

PLATFORM

XVIII. 1999 track diagram.

56.   Looking south we see Peckett 0-4-0ST *Merlin* and the path taken by visitors. They passed through the building on the right, under the bridge and along the path featured in the previous view. The gate marks the end of the running line. (V.Mitchell)

57.　　Recorded from near the platform end in August 1996 is the 1939 Peckett 0-4-0ST no. 1371 *Merlin*. Beyond the wagon is ex-NCB Barclay 0-4-0ST no. 22 and ex-BR diesel no. 03152. The signal box has 26 levers and was built by the LMS for Claydon, on the Bletchley-Oxford line, in 1941. (M.J.Stretton)

58.　　Adding to the variety of rolling stock on the SCR in 1996 were two coaches from Norwegian State Railways. They were intended for static use for catering purposes and are on isolated track in the yard. (M.J.Stretton)

Locomotive Stock on site at 31.12.1999

Steam

RICHARD TREVITHICK　0-4-0ST　　　A. Barclay 2354 of 1954
SWORDFISH 0-6-0ST　　　A. Barclay 2138 of 1941
0-6-0T　　Hudswell, Clarke 1857 of 1952
SLOUGH ESTATES No. 3 0-6-0ST　　　Hudswell, Clarke 1544 of 1924
FOREMARKE HALL 4-6-0　　　Swindon 1949
3845 2-8-0　　　Swindon 1942

Diesel

03152 0-6-0 Diesel Mechanical Swindon 1960
2022 0-6-0 Diesel Mechanical Swindon 1958
WOODBINE 0-4-0 Diesel Mechanical J. Fowler 21442 of 1936
0-4-0 Diesel Mechanical J. Fowler 4210137 of 1958
13261 0-6-0 Diesel Electric Derby 1956
0-4-0 Diesel Mechanical J. Fowler 4220031 of 1964
ARMY 9031 4w Petrol Trolley Wickham 8089 of 1958

MOREDON HALT

59.   The 40 ft long platform was opened on 25th March 1913, principally for milk traffic. There were often 25 churns waiting here. It did not appear in public timetables, but some passengers were known to use it until it closed on 1st October 1932. This southward view from 1934 includes the loop and points used for power station traffic. Receipts dropped from £845 in 1923 to £648 in 1931. (Mowat coll.)

XIX.   Although the loop was laid in 1923, the Swindon Corporation Electricity Works' sidings did not come into use until 17th January 1928. A petrol engined locomotive was employed until 1941, when a battery-electric machine arrived. The weigh bridge and coal receiving hoppers are on the horizontal line.

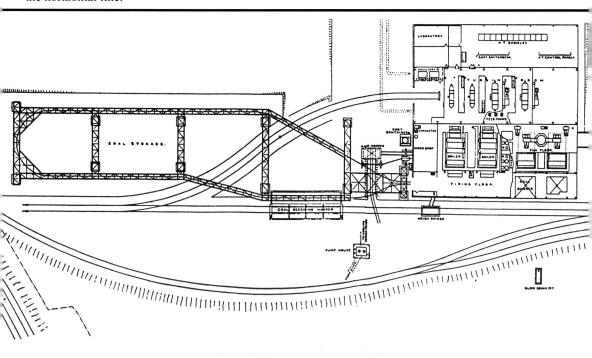

60.   Although coal supply to the power station ceased in about 1969, the track remained in place for around five years in anticipation of fuel oil traffic.   The line to Swindon Town runs diagonally across the picture, from left to right, and is seen during unseasonal floods on 18th July 1968. (Wiltshire Newspapers)

61.   This southward view from the road bridge shows the commencement of the sidings in April 1965. The power station ceased generating in March 1973 and its landmark chimney was felled on 1st March 1979 during the demolition process. (C.G.Maggs)

RUSHEY PLATT

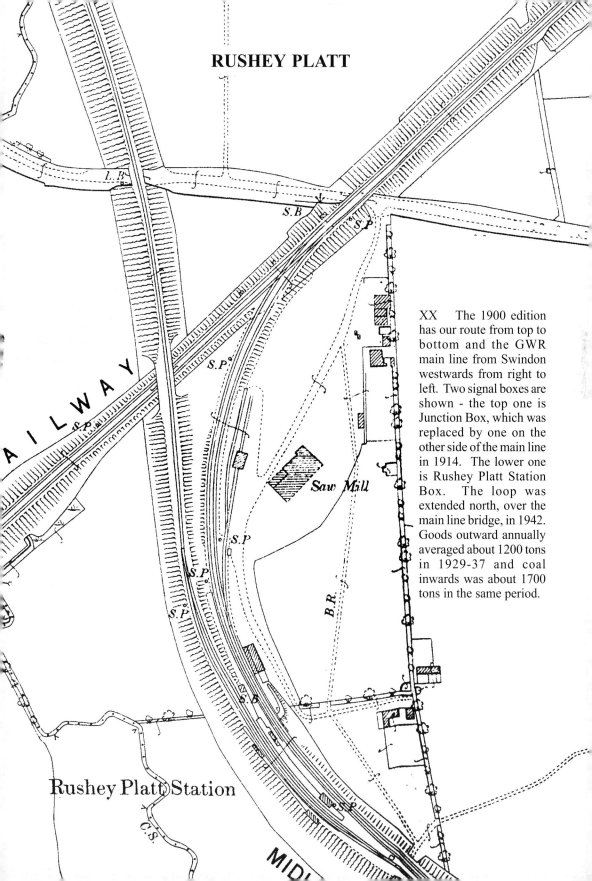

L.B.

S.B.

S.P.

S.P.

RAILWAY

S.P.

Saw Mill

S.P.

S.P.

S.P.

B.R.

S.B.

Rushey Platt Station

C.S.

S.P.

MIDL

XX   The 1900 edition has our route from top to bottom and the GWR main line from Swindon westwards from right to left. Two signal boxes are shown - the top one is Junction Box, which was replaced by one on the other side of the main line in 1914. The lower one is Rushey Platt Station Box. The loop was extended north, over the main line bridge, in 1942. Goods outward annually averaged about 1200 tons in 1929-37 and coal inwards was about 1700 tons in the same period.

62.   Part of the GWR's massive Swindon Works is on the left as we look through the telephone wires of the MSWJR route and along the 1841 main line in 1953. The curve on the right carried no passenger trains between 1885 and 1923, owing to uneconomic access charges being made by the GWR. The box was in use from 1914 to 1968, but a single line to Swindon Town was retained until 1975. (H.F.Wheeller/R.S.Carpenter)

63.	The original station was similar to those seen further north. It served as the northern terminus of the SMAR for three months, until the GWR completed the junction in February 1882. It is seen in 1953, with a southbound light engine in the background. The map shows that there was once a subway near the huts. (H.F.Wheeller/R.S.Carpenter)

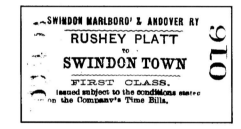

64.	The south end of the connection is on the right, as is one of the two platforms that were in use until 2nd March 1885. The two higher platforms were closed on 1st October 1905. The signal box which was of LSWR design was open from 1917 to 4th June 1965. It had 30 levers (6 spare), whereas its predecessor had only 18. (LGRP/NRM)

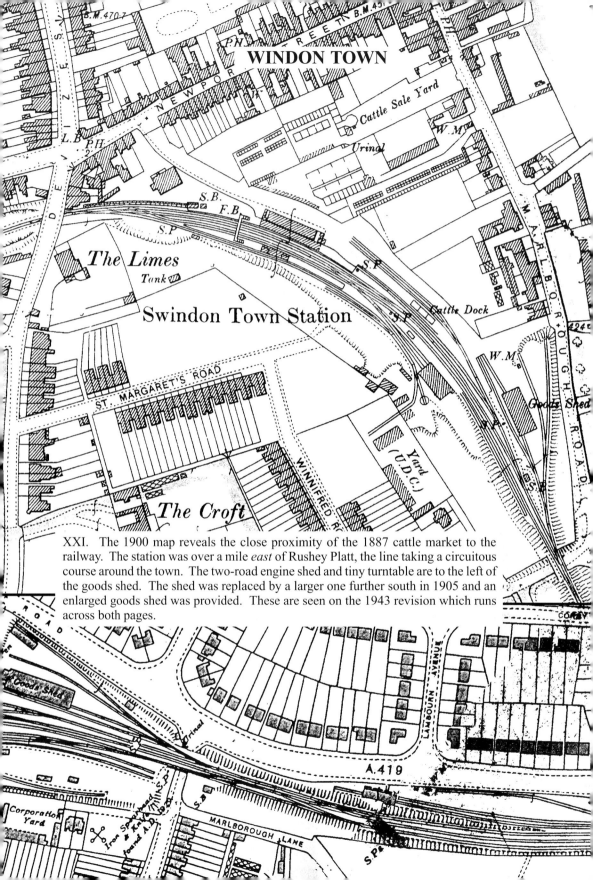

WINDON TOWN

Cattle Sale Yard

Urinal

The Limes

Tank

Swindon Town Station

Cattle Dock

Goods Shed

St. Margaret's Road

Winnifred Rd

Yard
(U.D.C.)

The Croft

XXI. The 1900 map reveals the close proximity of the 1887 cattle market to the railway. The station was over a mile *east* of Rushey Platt, the line taking a circuitous course around the town. The two-road engine shed and tiny turntable are to the left of the goods shed. The shed was replaced by a larger one further south in 1905 and an enlarged goods shed was provided. These are seen on the 1943 revision which runs across both pages.

Goods Shd

Corporation
Yard

MARLBOROUGH LANE

A.419

LAMBOURN AVENUE

65. This was one of only two stations on the MSWJR to have three platforms, but their curvature created an operating problem. Initially there had been three tracks between two platforms and there was a footbridge linking them from 1885. The arrangement seen in this eastward view dates from 1905. The shuttle train to Swindon Junction used the platform on the right. There was a staff of about 23 in the 1930s. Tickets issued dropped from 65,000 in 1923 to 28,000 in 1938, but season tickets increased from 12 to 80. (Lens of Sutton)

66. Allocated to Swindon Town in 1923 were two 0-6-0s, a 2-4-0, a 4-4-0 and 2-6-0 no 16. Photographed two years earlier, this engine was one of two elegant, simple and powerful machines purchased from Beyer Peacock for long distance freight work. This type was produced in large quantities for export, while most UK railways built their own and their designers did likewise to their egos. No. 16 served its owners well from 1897 to 1930. (LGRP/NRM)

67.   The two 1881 signal boxes were replaced by two of LSWR pattern in 1905; this is "A" Box, which had 17 levers and is seen in about 1935. The splendid building on the right was built as the general offices of the SMAR but, in the later years of the MSWJR, engineering matters were dealt with at Cirencester. It was closed in 1924 and is now used by a firm of accountants. (C.R.Clinker)

68. A railtour on 9th May 1953 had a nostalgic reminder of the MSWJR in the form of the only survivor of its locomotive fleet. No. 1336 was built in 1894 by Dubs & Company, ran as no. 12 until rebuilt with a GWR boiler in 1924 and was scrapped in 1954, after 60 years of service. (N.W. Sprinks)

69.   We can now enjoy three pictures from 1st July 1961. U class No. 31613 is being turned on the 55 ft turntable, which was installed in the 1904-05 rebuilding period. Traffic was increasing greatly at that time. It was unusual to find the turntable so remote from the engine shed. (S.C.Nash.)

70.   With the cattle dock in the background, the same locomotive departs south at 4.52 pm and largely obscures the 140 ft long goods shed, which housed a 5-ton crane. General goods traffic ceased on 19th May 1964, but coal continued until 3rd November 1966. (S.C.Nash)

71.   Moving further south, we witness the same engine arriving with the 2.50 pm from Andover Junction and also gain a glimpse of the 27-lever "B" Box. Both boxes ceased to function on 9th March 1964. The area is now occupied by an industrial estate. Oil traffic continued to the Esso Depot until 1968 and the site came to life again in 1970-71 when stone trains arrived from Cranmore with material for the M4 construction. A railtour appeared in both 1971 and 1972. The refreshment room remained open until January 1965. (S.C.Nash)

72.   The locomotive shed was closed on 21st January 1924, became a bus garage and later served the oil industry. It is on the right page of the 1943 map and was photographed 1965. (C.G.Maggs)

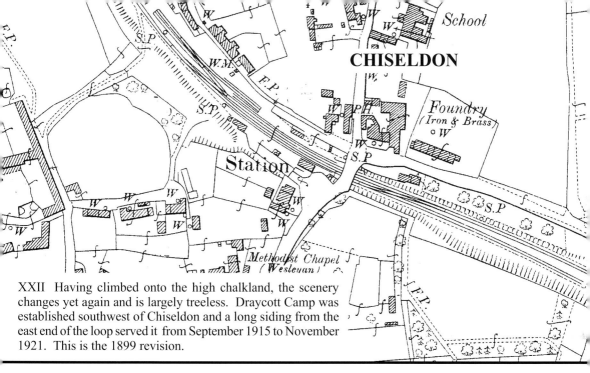

XXII Having climbed onto the high chalkland, the scenery changes yet again and is largely treeless. Draycott Camp was established southwest of Chiseldon and a long siding from the east end of the loop served it from September 1915 to November 1921. This is the 1899 revision.

73.   The village grew following the arrival of the railway, which always offered trains to and from Swindon to suit working hours. During wartime, the population increased greatly, which may account for the barrels in this undated southward view. In the final years, trains from Swindon terminated here at 8.17 am and 6.15 pm. (Lens of Sutton)

74.   Two horse boxes stand at the down platform and are a reminder that racehorse movement produced a substantial revenue here, due to the nearby training stables. Cart horses wait to move their next load of domestic coal from the yard. This traffic dropped from 1085 tons in 1923 to 469 in 1938, while tickets issued fell from 37,000 to 22,000. However, there were still over 300 season tickets sold. (Lens of Sutton)

75.   The original 20-lever signal box was replaced by this one in 1942, but the original base had been extended for it. The new frame controlled a second up loop, which was created south of the station on the trackbed of the Draycott Camp branch.This had run parallel to the running line for about half a mile. A 4300 class 2-6-0, no. 6334, is shunting on 15th March 1958. Beyond the box is a goods shed, which was erected in 1920. (H.C.Casserley)

76.   Bidirectional running had been practised since 8th February 1952, when it became possible to switch the signal box out of use. No. 6327 is piloted by no. 6395 on the last day of operation, 9th September 1961. The parcels office is beyond the signal box. (I.D.Beale)

CHISELDON CAMP HALT

77.   Draycott Camp had been named after a farm and was known as Chiseldon Camp by 1930, when a halt was opened on the west side of the line on 1st December. Unlike the station, it had electric lighting. Over 1000 tickets were issued in each of the first three years. A loop and siding   were provided north of it from 1943 to 1950. The well tended permanent way is seen in 1961. (Stations UK)

OGBOURNE

XXIII The population of the village was only 421 by 1961, probably little changed since this map was produced in 1900. Another large military camp was established about one mile west of the station, but traffic was about 10% of that at Chiseldon. There was once a private siding for stables at Ogbourne St. Andrew, 1½ miles south of the station.

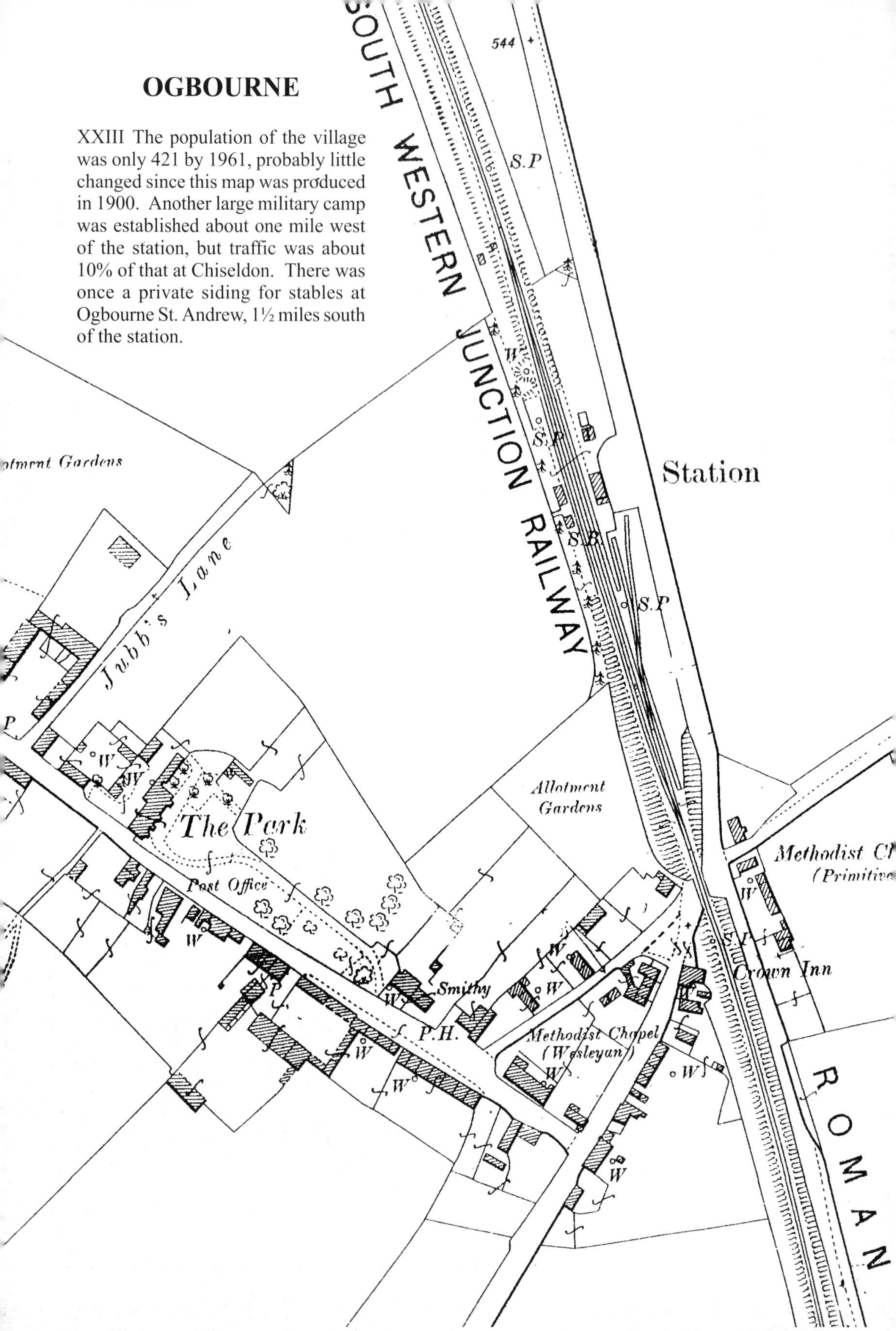

544 +

S.P

SOUTH WESTERN JUNCTION RAILWAY

Station

S.P

S.B

S.P

otment Gardens

Jubb's Lane

Allotment Gardens

The Park

Methodist C⁰ (Primitive

Post Office

Crown Inn

Smithy

P.H.

Methodist Chapel (Wesleyan)

ROMAN

78.   The 10.0am Cheltenham Lansdown to Andover Junction was hauled by 4-6-0 no. 7808 *Cookham Manor* on 24th September 1956. The locomotive now resides at the Didcot Railway Centre. The signal box on the left was replaced by the one in the distance on 7th January 1943, due to loop lengthening. The old box was retained as an office for the Permanent Way Dept. (H.C.Casserley)

79.   This southward view is from July 1961. The A345 passed behind the building and under the track, just beyond the points. It now follows the route of the railway and bypasses the village. The sidings are concealed by grass; they remained usable until the complete closure of this section of the route on 11th September 1961. The platform on the right was seldom used, as the tracks were bidirectional. (J.J.Smith)

MARLBOROUGH

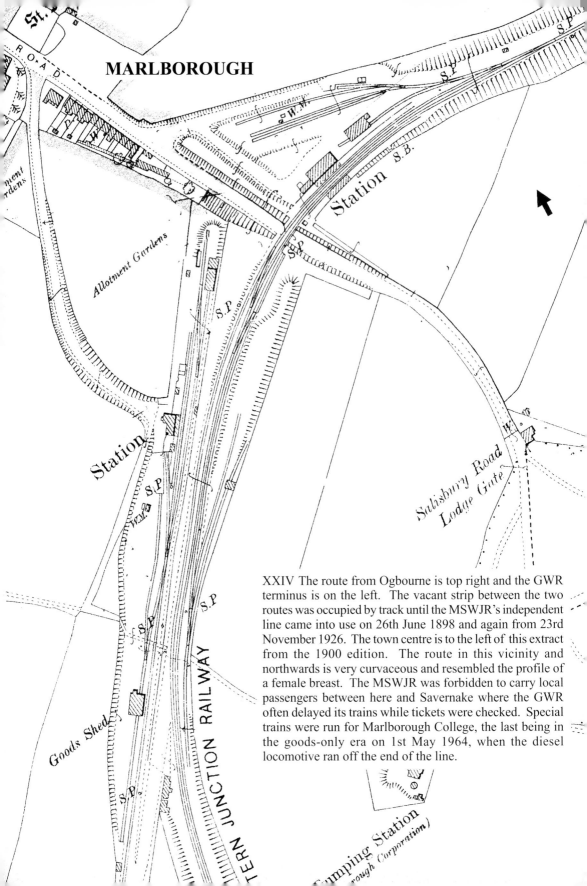

XXIV The route from Ogbourne is top right and the GWR terminus is on the left. The vacant strip between the two routes was occupied by track until the MSWJR's independent line came into use on 26th June 1898 and again from 23rd November 1926. The town centre is to the left of this extract from the 1900 edition. The route in this vicinity and northwards is very curvaceous and resembled the profile of a female breast. The MSWJR was forbidden to carry local passengers between here and Savernake where the GWR often delayed its trains while tickets were checked. Special trains were run for Marlborough College, the last being in the goods-only era on 1st May 1964, when the diesel locomotive ran off the end of the line.

80.　　Postern Hill and the popular Savernake Forest are on the right in this eastward view, which includes the MSWJR signal box which was in use until 15th February 1933. Its successor was built near the points to the 1888 horse dock siding seen on the right. The girders span the A346. (R.M.Casserley Coll.)

81.　　One of the popular 4500 2-6-2Ts waits to depart south, while three other locomotives stand in the goods yard, which did not have a headshunt until 1933. Servicemen are a reminder of the importance of military traffic on the route. Ticket sales dropped from 28,000 to 19,000 between 1923 and 1930, while goods tonnage handled rose from 8000 to 14,000; there were seven men employed here. (Lens of Sutton)

82.   Down goods trains could be held in the up platform, while a down passenger passed. One such goods train was hauled by 4300 class no. 6320 on 1st September 1952. The station was known as "Low Level" between 1924 and 1933. (H.C.Casserley)

83.   Ex-GWR 0-6-0PT no. 9605 is passing over the main road with the 12.38 pm (Sundays only) from Andover Junction to Swindon on 16th September 1956. The coaches are ex-LSWR. In the background is a wagon standing in the former GWR premises. Passenger traffic had ceased there on 6th March 1933, but goods continued until 19th May 1964. (S.C.Nash)

84.   The refreshment room on the left was added in 1884 and for long served as a "local". No. 9672 is carrying shedplate 82C, indicating that Swindon is its base. It is hauling the 1.5 pm Saturdays-only Swindon (Junction) to Savernake (Low Level), which was the only such working during the week. The date is 15th March 1958. (R.C.Riley)

SOUTH OF MARLBOROUGH

85.   The 1898 double track used by MSWJR trains was converted to two single lines on 6th March 1933. The western one was used for a local service to Savernake (Low Level) to connect with main line trains. No. 3666 is working the shuttle on 1st July 1961 and in the background is part of the 1864 branch of the GWR, which was retained as a headshunt for the goods yard referred to in caption 83. The eastern line runs to Savernake (High Level) and the flyover across the London line. (S.C.Nash)

NORTH OF SAVERNAKE

XXV. The diagram shows the situation in 1958, most of the GWR single line branch having been taken out of use in 1933. North-south services could use either station at Savernake; in 1958, two used Low Level and three High Level. The latter number was in a legal agreement made in 1898 with the local landowner.

86. To take a more direct route than the GWR branch, the MSWJR required a 648 yd long tunnel. This is the southern portal in 1960. Major repairs were required on two occasions and the cuttings were always prone to chalk fall, which had to be cleared every winter. (J.J.Smith)

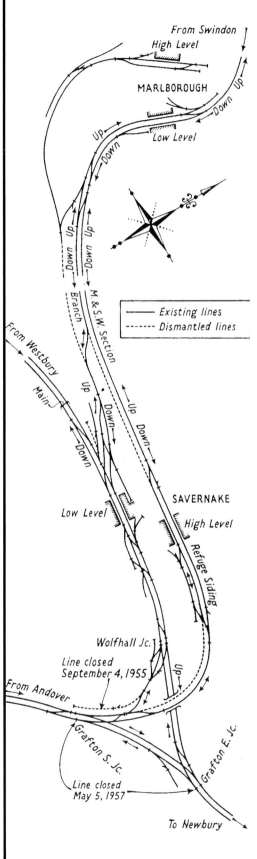

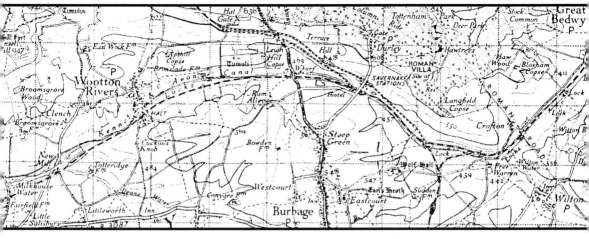

XXVI. The 1 ins to 1 mile map of 1934 indicates that the two single tracks diverged more than a mile before reaching the Savernake stations. Our route runs from top to bottom.

87.   Two miles south of Marlborough Tunnel, a siding ran northeast into Savernake Ordnance Depot from 18th August 1943 to 27th August 1950. A violent explosion occurred on 2nd January 1946, which killed eight soldiers, injured many more and destroyed 29 wagons, together with three lorries. Captain Biggs and Sergeant Rogerson received GCs for moving burning wagons and motivating the survivors to act to prevent more than 2000 tons of shells and mines exploding. They worked all night and saved 69 loaded wagons, while propellants exploded around them. Many fires were still burning next day when this picture was taken; the firefighters also received a number of medals. Thus local life and property was preserved. A less serious train fire had occurred late in 1943. (S.Rogerson)

SAVERNAKE

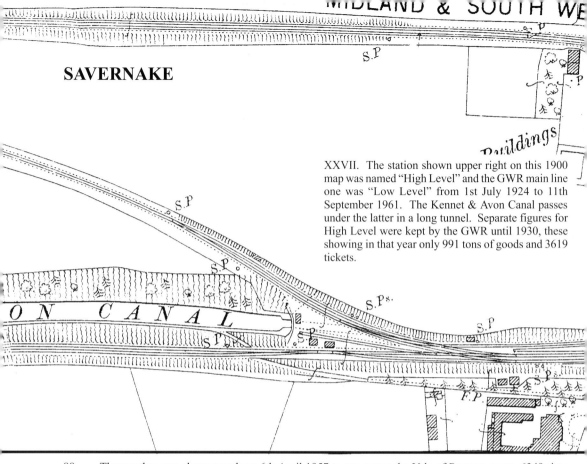

XXVII. The station shown upper right on this 1900 map was named "High Level" and the GWR main line one was "Low Level" from 1st July 1924 to 11th September 1961. The Kennet & Avon Canal passes under the latter in a long tunnel. Separate figures for High Level were kept by the GWR until 1930, these showing in that year only 991 tons of goods and 3619 tickets.

88.   The weather was clear enough on 6th April 1957 to see across the Vale of Pewsey, as no. 6349 rises from it and enters the High Level up platform with the 4.36 pm Southampton Terminus to Cheltenham Spa Lansdown. There had been no less than eight boxes in the Savernake area; this one had become "High Level Middle Ground Frame" in 1933. It had the usual 14 lever frame. Goods traffic ceased on the sidings in the foreground on 22nd June 1959. (N.W.Sprinks)

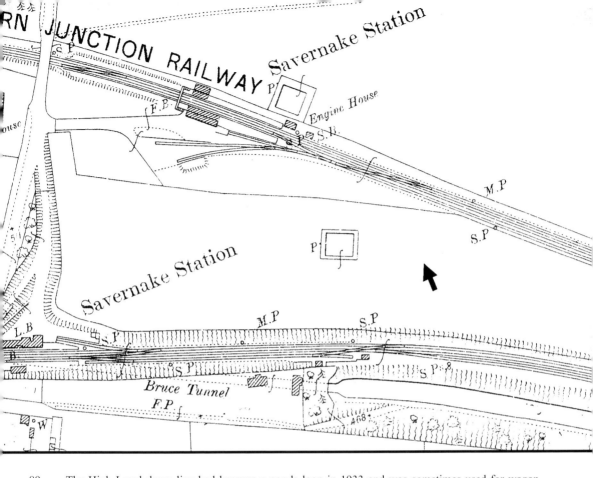

89.   The High Level down line had become a goods loop in 1933 and was sometimes used for wagon storage, as seen on 6th July 1959. The building on the right had been the private waiting room of the Marquis of Ailesbury, who had leased land in Savernake Forest to the MSWJR. The main building is now in use as a dwelling. (R.M.Casserley)

90.   The Low Level station always had a passing loop, but it was not until 1899 that the main line was doubled. The Marlborough bay is on the left as 0-6-0PT no. 9790 takes water on 6th July 1959, while working the 2.50 pm Andover Junction to Swindon Town. This station was closed to goods traffic on 19th May 1964 and to passengers on 18th April 1966. (H.C.Casserley)

91.   The 1898 line to the High Level is in the centre background as the 1.52 pm from Cheltenham Spa St. James joins the main line and enters the Low Level up platform on 3rd June 1961. Local trains for Marlborough departed from the bay on the right and climbed the curve in the centre background. (E.Wilmshurst)

92.   U class no. 31629 runs between Grafton South Junction and Wolfhall Junction with the 2.50 pm from Andover Junction on 18th July 1959. These locations are shown on the diagram near picture 86. The bridge on the right is over the canal and the one on the left carried the ex-MSWJR route over the main line. Behind the camera was Wolfhall Junction Box, which was in use until 22nd November 1964. Through running ceased from 1898 to 1902. (J.J.Smith)

93.   No. 31801 is southbound on the same day and is at Grafton South Junction, with the 1905 Grafton Curve on the right. This did not carry regular passenger services and had been closed on 5th May 1957. The box also controlled the junction of the High Level and Low Level lines, the signal for which is on the left. The box was open until passenger services ceased. (J.J.Smith)

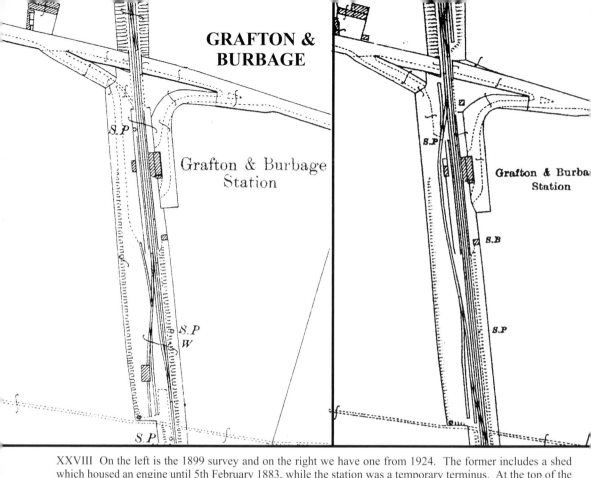

GRAFTON & BURBAGE

Grafton & Burbage
Station

Grafton & Burba:
Station

XXVIII On the left is the 1899 survey and on the right we have one from 1924. The former includes a shed which housed an engine until 5th February 1883, while the station was a temporary terminus. At the top of the later edition are two sidings that were added in 1902. Curving from the eastern one was a two-mile long siding to Dodsdown Brickworks, which was in use until 1910. The firm had a Peckett 0-6-0ST, followed by an 0-4-0ST new from the same builder in 1907. There was one level crossing at Heath Lane.

94.   The 18-lever MSWJR box remained in use until line closure in 1961 and was photographed in 1956. The line northwards was doubled in 1898, when Savernake (High Level) came into use. From 1923 to 1938, total receipts dropped from £10,582 to £856, staffing increased from 4 to 6, while freight tonnage went from 8644 to 1975. (R.C.Riley)

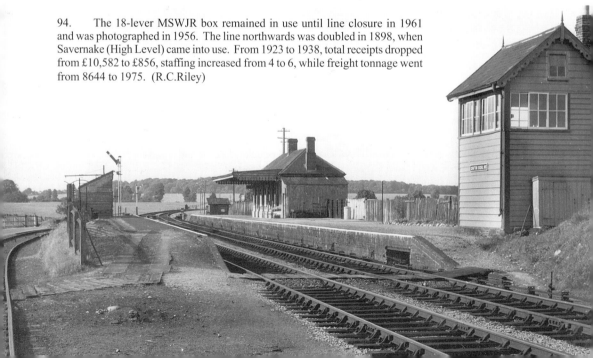

95. The 2.50 pm Andover Junction to Swindon Town was headed by 0-6-0PT no. 9790 on 6th July 1959. The goods yard remained open until the line closed. The area was thinly populated. The route was doubled southward to Collingbourne on 2nd November 1902. A camping coach was located here in 1941 to house workers involved in adapting Malmesbury Common for food production. (H.C.Casserley)

96. The RCTS special train was recorded on the last day of the line, 9th September 1961. Note that Southern Region upper quadrant signals had appeared since the line southwards had been transferred to it in 1950. (I.D.Beale)

COLLINGBOURNE KINGSTON HALT

97. The halt was opened on 1st April 1932 and was close to the village, being south of the lane to Brunton. There was no foot crossing, as there was access to both platforms from the road. Tickets were available from a house on the main road and around 1500 were sold each year in the 1930s. (E.Wilmshurst)

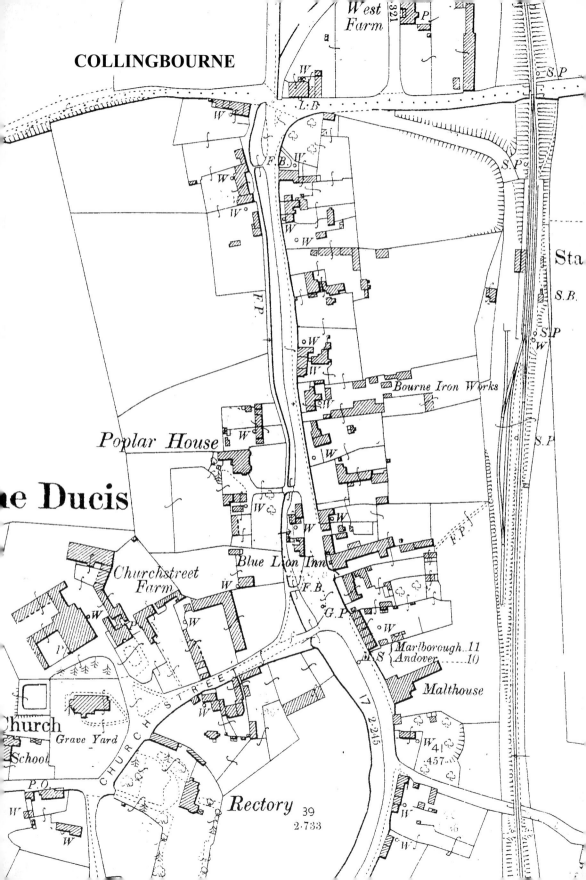

COLLINGBOURNE

West
Farm
321

S.P.

L.B.

F.B.

S.P.

F.P.

Sta

S.B.

S.P.

W

Bourne Iron Works

Poplar House

W

e Ducis

W

Blue Lion Inn

F.B.

Churchstreet
Farm

G.P.

W

Marlborough..11
S Andover.......10

Malthouse

CHURCH STREET

17
2.245

W 41
.457

Church

Grave Yard

School

P.O.

Rectory   39
2.733

XXIX. The station was well situated in relation to the village of Collingbourne Ducis, but the local population of about 1000 was widely spread. A short dock siding was added north of the up platform in 1906 and the yard was altered to simply have two parallel sidings, soon after this survey was made in 1899.

98. U class no. 31626 is approaching one small passenger and two small churns. The original building remained in use, little changed, throughout the life of the line, but there is evidence of platform lengthening. (H.F.Wheeller/R.S.Carpenter)

99. The same train departs south on 27th May 1961, on the line that was doubled on 1st September 1901; it is climbing at 1 in 100. The simplified layout of the yard is evident. A staff of three in the 1930s saw freight tonnage drop from over 5000 to under 3000, although there was a peak of 10,308 in 1933 due to stone arriving for road improvements. Ticket figures dropped similarly. (H.F.Wheeller/R.S.Carpenter)

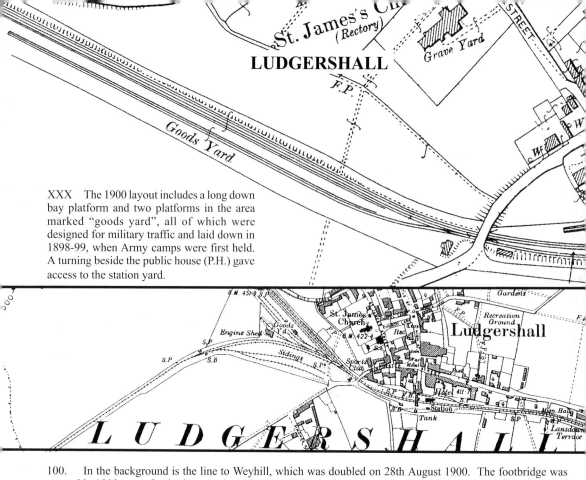

XXX   The 1900 layout includes a long down bay platform and two platforms in the area marked "goods yard", all of which were designed for military traffic and laid down in 1898-99, when Army camps were first held. A turning beside the public house (P.H.) gave access to the station yard.

100.   In the background is the line to Weyhill, which was doubled on 28th August 1900. The footbridge was erected in 1902, one of only three on the MSWJR. Wide platforms were provided for assembly and marching of troops. (Lens of Sutton)

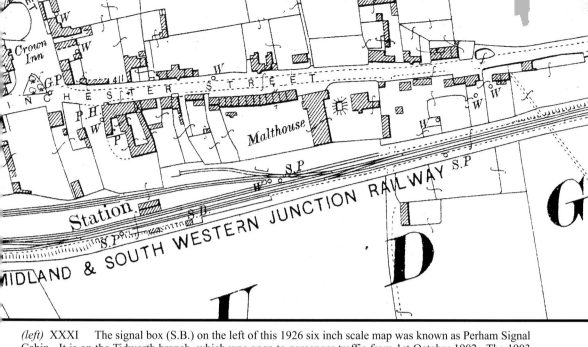

(left) XXXI   The signal box (S.B.) on the left of this 1926 six inch scale map was known as Perham Signal
Cabin. It is on the Tidworth branch, which was open to passenger traffic from 1st October 1902. The 1903
branch engine shed is shown, as is the 1902 good shed and the 55ft turntable. The two sidings to the south of
them date from 1916. The engine shed was closed in July 1925 and the public goods yard on 24th March 1964.
A 5-ton crane had been available.

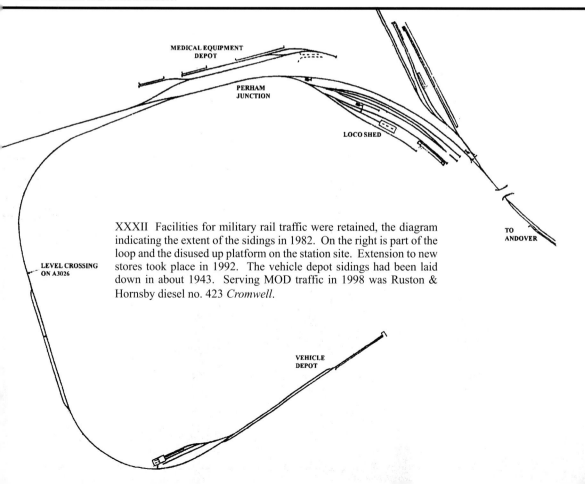

XXXII Facilities for military rail traffic were retained, the diagram
indicating the extent of the sidings in 1982. On the right is part of the
loop and the disused up platform on the station site. Extension to new
stores took place in 1992. The vehicle depot sidings had been laid
down in about 1943. Serving MOD traffic in 1998 was Ruston &
Hornsby diesel no. 423 *Cromwell*.

101.   The booking office was built during 1900 but does not show on the map. The bowler hat by the step belongs to the gentleman attending King George V on 8th November 1917. The rear of the Royal Train can be seen in the down bay. (Lens of Sutton)

102.   The ticket office was in the main building until 1900, and again from 1908. Passengers were supposed to use the footbridge and not this crossing over the siding, which was photographed in 1952. Tickets issued declined from 29,000 in 1923 to 20,000 in 1938, staff levels dropping from 16 to 12, but freight increased from 8000 to 14,000 tons over the same period. (H.C.Casserley)

103.   Perham Signal Cabin was devoid of its nameplate when photographed in July 1956, as it had closed in 1955. Some of its eleven levers were used as a ground frame. Alongside is WD no. 831 and in the background is the water tank and goods shed. (R.C.Riley)

104.   The 1901 signal box was of LSWR design and had 40 levers. The bay on the right for the Tidworth branch train was also from 1901. The double line to Perham Cabin was singled in 1955. There was no freight for 2-8-0 no. 2887 to take to Swindon on 3rd June 1961. The line to Andover had been singled on 29th August 1960. (E Wilmshurst)

105. The northern part of the station site was cleared for housing, leaving just a loop and fragments of platform. Five return trips from Andover were operated on 23rd March 1983, giving a rare opportunity to traverse the lines. No. 4930 *Hagley Hall* is reversing its train into the loop.
(E. Wilmshurst)

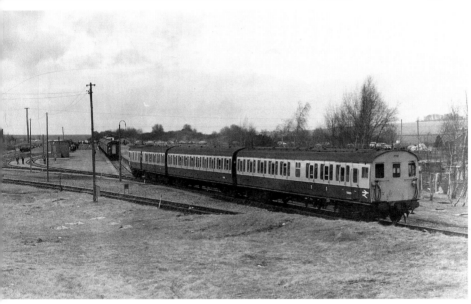

106. The train seen in the previous picture stands at what was still known as "Horse Platform", while DEMU no. 1110 reverses from it to take enthusiasts on a short trip on the remains of the Tidworth branch. It would soon run forward on the line in the foreground. The compound was used in the 1990s for storing redundant BR stock, notably class 33 diesels.
(E Wilmshurst)

107. Seen from almost the same viewpoint as picture 106 is Perham Yard and the MOD locomotive shed, on 27th August 1998. Traffic increased following the provision of a direct rail link with Germany under the Channel and another surge occurred during the Balkans conflict in 1999.
(V. Mitchell)

TIDWORTH

108. The extensive barracks are in the background of this westward view. Tented Summer camps for up to 30,000 men were held in the early years,but a permanent camp grew steadily as a result of the MSWJR conveying millions of bricks from Grafton. (Lens of Sutton)

109. Provision was made for long troop trains and both platforms had water columns. The platform on the right was more than twice as long as those on the main line of the MSWJR, except Ludgershall. Goods outward had included horse manure to the strawberry beds of Hampshire and dog droppings to the tanneries of the Midlands. (Lens of Sutton)

110.   A 1952 panorama includes the 5-ton crane, the 26-lever signal box and the three starting signals. The engine release crossovers were so far from the box that they were worked from a four-lever ground frame. Public goods traffic ceased on 25th November 1955, when branch operation reverted to the Army. (H.C.Casserley)

XXXIII Started as a simple military siding in 1900 to serve new barracks associated with the demands of the Boer War (1899-1902), the branch was leased to the MSWJR, which began goods traffic on 1st July 1902 and carried passengers from 1st October of that year. The lines west of the station continued to be operated by the Army and, to the left of the word RAILWAY, a substantial bridge was provided over the main road, which is now the A338. The right of this map continues from the previous one. The camp railway closed in 1953, there having been about 2½ miles of track within its boundary.

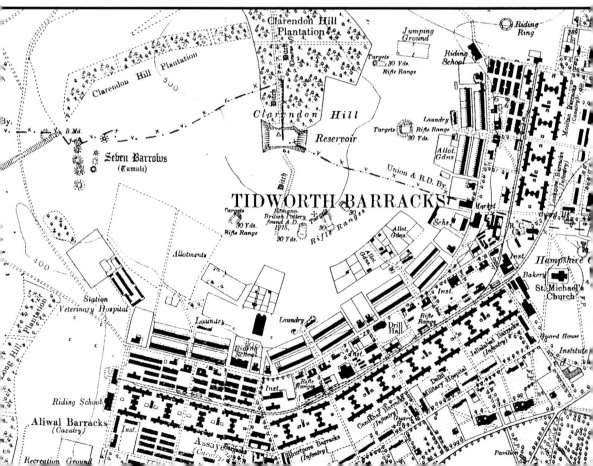

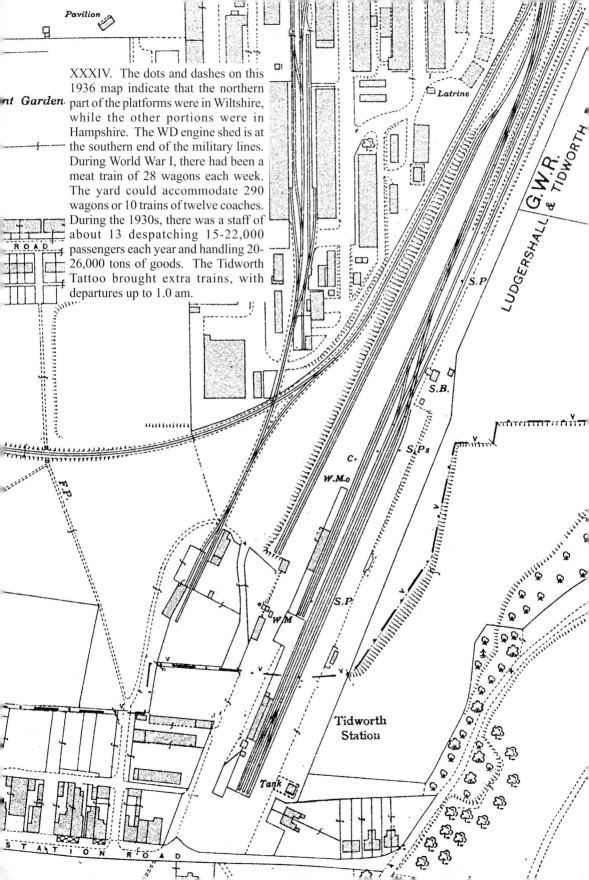

XXXIV. The dots and dashes on this 1936 map indicate that the northern part of the platforms were in Wiltshire, while the other portions were in Hampshire. The WD engine shed is at the southern end of the military lines. During World War I, there had been a meat train of 28 wagons each week. The yard could accommodate 290 wagons or 10 trains of twelve coaches. During the 1930s, there was a staff of about 13 despatching 15-22,000 passengers each year and handling 20-26,000 tons of goods. The Tidworth Tattoo brought extra trains, with departures up to 1.0 am.

Pavilion

nt Garden

ROAD

Latrine

G.W.R. & TIDWORTH

LUDGERSHALL

S.P.

S.B.

S.Ps

C.

W.M.

F.P.

W.M

S.P.

Tidworth Station

Tank

STATION ROAD

111.   Two ex-GWR coaches sufficed for many years, often hauled by a 4500 class 2-6-2T. Seen here is LMS designed 2-6-2T no. 41305, a regular performer subsequently. US Army forces were in the garrison in the 1942-46 period. The ground frame hut is on the left. (Lens of Sutton)

June 1952

Miles	TIDWORTH and LUDGERSHALL																														
	Week Days only																														
		a.m				p.m				p.m																					
—	Tidworth............. dep	7 50	..	..	..	12 15	..	:	..	4 45	..	:	..	:	..	:	..	:	..	:	..	:	..	:	..	"..	..	"..	..	"..	..
2¼	Ludgershall............. arr	7 57	..	..	..	12 22	..	:	..	4 52	..	:	..	:	..	:	..	:	..	:	..	:	..	:	..	"..	..	"..	..	"..	..

112.   In the final period of operation, ex-GWR 4300 class 2-6-0 no. 5396 was in use. It is seen on 17th September 1955, about to depart at 4.45 pm with the last passenger train. The branch was closed completely on 31st July 1963, the final troop train having run on 25th May 1962. (J.J.Smith)

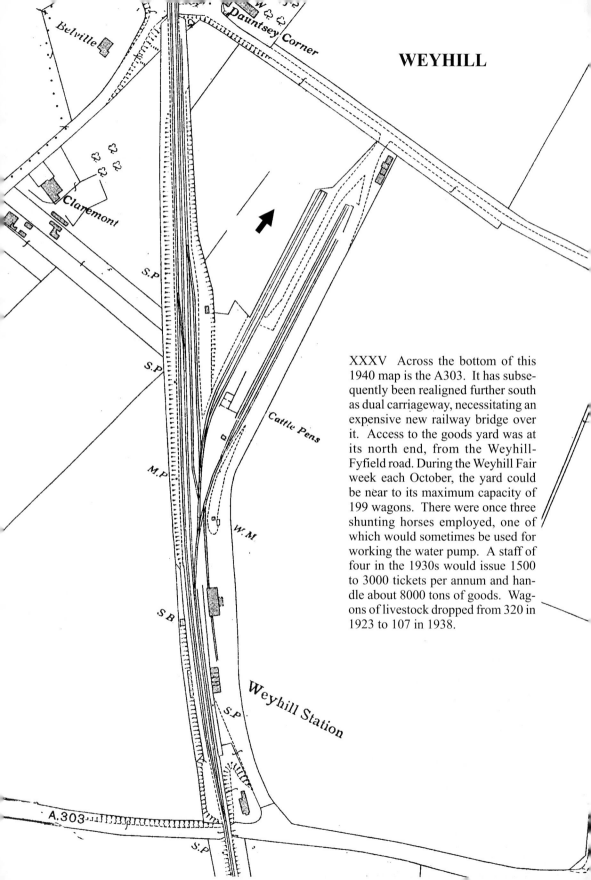

WEYHILL

Belville

Dauntsey Corner

Claremont

S.P

S.P

M.P

Cattle Pens

W.M

S.B

Weyhill Station

S.P

A.303

S.P

XXXV Across the bottom of this 1940 map is the A303. It has subsequently been realigned further south as dual carriageway, necessitating an expensive new railway bridge over it. Access to the goods yard was at its north end, from the Weyhill-Fyfield road. During the Weyhill Fair week each October, the yard could be near to its maximum capacity of 199 wagons. There were once three shunting horses employed, one of which would sometimes be used for working the water pump. A staff of four in the 1930s would issue 1500 to 3000 tickets per annum and handle about 8000 tons of goods. Wagons of livestock dropped from 320 in 1923 to 107 in 1938.

113.   As ex-GWR no. 6349 shunts on a gloomy day in July 1958, we gain a glimpse of the goods yard, which changed little from its opening in 1882 until its closure on 1st December 1969. The water tank and one-ton crane are visible, the latter having appeared during the 1930s. (R.C.Riley)

114.   A southward view in 1961 includes the iron goods shed, the redundant up track and the 20-lever box, which was closed when the line was singled. Lamps of the pressurised oil type were hoisted up the posts at night. (E. Wilmshurst)

115.   The 1900 double track from Ludgershall was singled on 29th August 1961, right through to Andover. Double track southwards had come into use on 5th September 1943 and a spur eastwards from the goods yards for the RAF was laid at about that time. The two sidings visible were usable until April 1981. (S.C.Nash)

RED POST JUNCTION

116.   The MSWJR was obliged to use a separate single line, parallel to the LSWR double track, into Andover. However, this was not possible for the first six months. From January 1919 to September 1936, there was a connection between the routes, the signal box being between them. The link was restored and this box was opened on 5th September 1943, as part of the preparations for the invasion of Europe. No. 31793 has rounded the curve with the 1.48 pm from Cheltenham Spa St. James on 27th August 1960 and the signalman awaits the token. The box closed on 1st September 1963 and the points were removed in 1966. (J.J.Smith)

ANDOVER

117.   The station was "Andover Junction" from 1865 to 1964; the north side of it (left) and the land carrying the single track from Red Post Junction belonged to the MSWJR until 1912. West Box is on the right and East Box is in the distance; both were in use from 1882 to 1973. (Lens of Sutton)

118.   The MSWJR had its own engine shed, which is in the left background of the previous picture and which was allocated a 4-4-0, a 4-4-4T, an 0-6-0T and an 0-4-4T in 1923. Seen in April 1928 is no. 1126, one of eight 4-4-0s built for the MSWJR in 1905-14 and numbered 8 in their fleet. (H.C.Casserley)

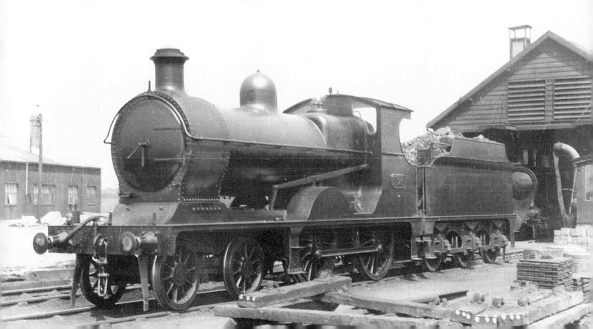

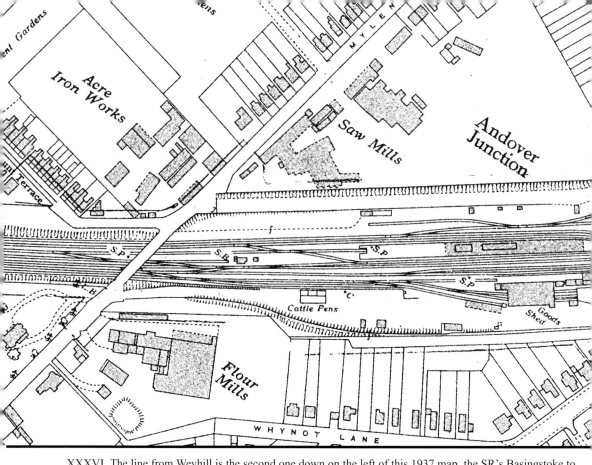

XXXVI The line from Weyhill is the second one down on the left of this 1937 map, the SR's Basingstoke to Salisbury route runs from right to left and the line to Romsey is lower right. Trains to Southampton used this route until 7th September 1964. SR engines used the shed north of the turntable and GWR locos were housed in the one to the south. They closed in 1962 and 1958 respectively, the site later being redeveloped as a fertiliser store.

119.   The 2.35 pm to Swindon Town was hauled by ex-GWR no. 7312 on 6th April 1957. There were only four other departures north at this time. The line next to the train could be used for through running to Southampton. (N.W.Sprinks)

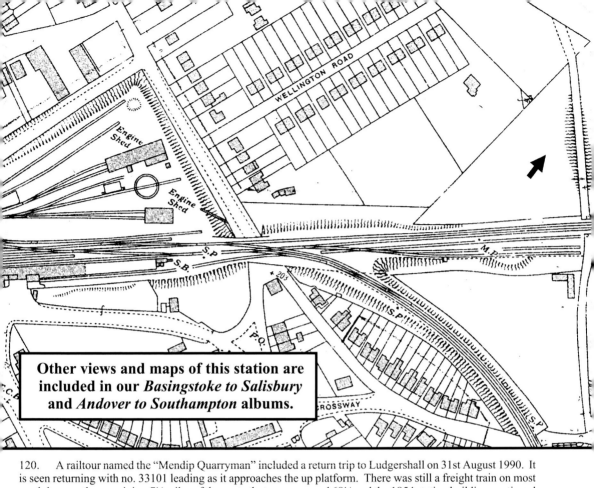

Other views and maps of this station are included in our *Basingstoke to Salisbury* and *Andover to Southampton* albums.

120. A railtour named the "Mendip Quarryman" included a return trip to Ludgershall on 31st August 1990. It is seen returning with no. 33101 leading as it approaches the up platform. There was still a freight train on most weekdays on the remaining 7½ miles of the route that once covered 68½ and the 1854 station building continued to serve travellers using South West Trains. (M. Turvey)

Middleton Press

Easebourne Lane, Midhurst, W Sussex. GU29 9AZ Tel: 01730 813169 Fax: 01730 812601
If books are not available from your local transport stockist, order direct with cheque,
Visa or Mastercard, post free UK.

BRANCH LINES
Branch Line to Allhallows
Branch Line to Alton
Branch Lines around Ascot
Branch Line to Ashburton
Branch Lines around Bodmin
Branch Line to Bude
Branch Lines around Canterbury
Branch Lines around Chard & Yeovil
Branch Line to Cheddar
Branch Lines around Cromer
Branch Lines of East London
Branch Lines to Effingham Junction
Branch Lines around Exmouth
Branch Line to Fairford
Branch Lines around Gosport
Branch Line to Hawkhurst
Branch Line to Hayling
Branch Lines to Horsham
Branch Lines around Huntingdon
Branch Line to Kingswear
Branch Lines to Launceston & Princetown
Branch Lines to Longmoor
Branch Line to Looe
Branch Line to Lyme Regis
Branch Lines around March
Branch Lines around Midhurst
Branch Line to Minehead
Branch Line to Moretonhampstead
Branch Lines to Newport (IOW)
Branch Line to Padstow
Branch Lines around Plymouth
Branch Lines to Seaton and Sidmouth
Branch Line to Selsey
Branch Lines around Sheerness
Branch Line to Shrewsbury
Branch Line to Swanage *updated*
Branch Line to Tenterden
Branch Lines to Torrington
Branch Lines to Tunbridge Wells
Branch Line to Upwell
Branch Lines around Weymouth
Branch Lines around Wimborne
Branch Lines around Wisbech

NARROW GAUGE BRANCH LINES
Branch Line to Lynton
Branch Lines around Portmadoc 1923-46
Branch Lines around Porthmadog 1954-94
Branch Line to Southwold
Two-Foot Gauge Survivors
Romneyrail
Vivarais Narrow Gauge

SOUTH COAST RAILWAYS
Ashford to Dover
Bournemouth to Weymouth
Brighton to Eastbourne
Brighton to Worthing
Chichester to Portsmouth
Dover to Ramsgate
Eastbourne to Hastings
Hastings to Ashford
Portsmouth to Southampton
Southampton to Bournemouth
Worthing to Chichester

SOUTHERN MAIN LINES
Basingstoke to Salisbury
Bromley South to Rochester
Crawley to Littlehampton
Dartford to Sittingbourne
East Croydon to Three Bridges
Epsom to Horsham

Exeter to Barnstaple
Exeter to Tavistock
Faversham to Dover
London Bridge to East Croydon
Orpington to Tonbridge
Tonbridge to Hastings
Salisbury to Yeovil
Swanley to Ashford
Tavistock to Plymouth
Victoria to East Croydon
Waterloo to Windsor
Waterloo to Woking
Woking to Portsmouth
Woking to Southampton
Yeovil to Exeter

EASTERN MAIN LINES
Fenchurch Street to Barking
Ipswich to Saxmundham
Liverpool Street to Ilford

WESTERN MAIN LINES
Ealing to Slough
Paddington to Ealing

COUNTRY RAILWAY ROUTES
Andover to Southampton
Bath Green Park to Bristol
Bath to Evercreech Junction
Bournemouth to Evercreech Jn.
Cheltenham to Andover
Croydon to East Grinstead
Didcot to Winchester
East Kent Light Railway
Fareham to Salisbury
Frome to Bristol
Guildford to Redhill
Porthmadog to Blaenau
Reading to Basingstoke
Reading to Guildford
Redhill to Ashford
Salisbury to Westbury
Stratford upon Avon to Cheltenham
Strood to Paddock Wood
Taunton to Barnstaple
Wenford Bridge to Fowey
Westbury to Bath
Woking to Alton
Yeovil to Dorchester

GREAT RAILWAY ERAS
Ashford from Steam to Eurostar
Clapham Junction 50 years of change
Festiniog in the Fifties
Festiniog in the Sixties
Isle of Wight Lines 50 years of change
Railways to Victory 1944-46
SECR Centenary album
Talyllyn 50 years of change
Yeovil 50 years of change

LONDON SUBURBAN RAILWAYS
Caterham and Tattenham Corner
Charing Cross to Dartford
Clapham Jn. to Beckenham Jn.
East London Line
Finsbury Park to Alexandra Palace
Kingston and Hounslow Loops
Lewisham to Dartford
Lines around Wimbledon
London Bridge to Addiscombe
Mitcham Junction Lines
North London Line
South London Line

West Croydon to Epsom
West London Line
Willesden Junction to Richmond
Wimbledon to Epsom

STEAMING THROUGH
Steaming through Cornwall
Steaming through Kent
Steaming through West Hants
Steaming through West Sussex

TRAMWAY CLASSICS
Aldgate & Stepney Tramways
Barnet & Finchley Tramways
Bath Tramways
Bournemouth & Poole Tramways
Brighton's Tramways
Camberwell & W.Norwood Tramways
Clapham & Streatham Tramways
Dover's Tramways
East Ham & West Ham Tramways
Edgware and Willesden Tramways
Eltham & Woolwich Tramways
Embankment & Waterloo Tramways
Enfield & Wood Green Tramways
Exeter & Taunton Tramways
Gosport & Horndean Tramways
Greenwich & Dartford Tramways
Hammersmith & Hounslow Tramways
Hampstead & Highgate Tramways
Hastings Tramways
Holborn & Finsbury Tramways
Ilford & Barking Tramways
Kingston & Wimbledon Tramways
Lewisham & Catford Tramways
Liverpool Tramways 1. Eastern Routes
Liverpool Tramways 2. Southern Routes
Maidstone & Chatham Tramways
North Kent Tramways
Norwich Tramways
Portsmouth's Tramways
Reading Tramways
Seaton & Eastbourne Tramways
Shepherds Bush & Uxbridge Tramways
Southampton Tramways
Southend-on-sea Tramways
Southwark & Deptford Tramways
Stamford Hill Tramways
Twickenham & Kingston Tramways
Victoria & Lambeth Tramways
Waltham Cross & Edmonton Tramways
Walthamstow & Leyton Tramways
Wandsworth & Battersea Tramways

TROLLEYBUS CLASSICS
Croydon Trolleybuses
Bournemouth Trolleybuses
Hastings Trolleybuses
Maidstone Trolleybuses
Reading Trolleybuses
Woolwich & Dartford Trolleybuses

WATERWAY ALBUMS
Kent and East Sussex Waterways
London to Portsmouth Waterway
West Sussex Waterways

MILITARY BOOKS
Battle over Portsmouth
Battle over Sussex 1940
Blitz over Sussex 1941-42
Bombers over Sussex 1943-45
Bognor at War
Military Defence of West Sussex
Secret Sussex Resistance
Sussex Home Guard

OTHER RAILWAY BOOKS
Garraway Father & Son
Index to all Middleton Press stations
Industrial Railways of the South-East
South Eastern & Chatham Railways
London Chatham & Dover Railway
War on the Line (SR 1939-45)